T0104581

The Journey

Navigating Your Teenage Years

MORRIS GLEISER

Scripture taken from the King James Version of the Bible.

WestBow Press books may be ordered through booksellers or by contacting:

WestBow Press
A Division of Thomas Nelson & Zondervan
1663 Liberty Drive
Bloomington, IN 47403
www.westbowpress.com
1 (866) 928-1240

ISBN: 978-1-4908-9122-4 (sc)
ISBN: 978-1-4908-9124-8 (hc)
ISBN: 978-1-4908-9123-1 (e)

Print information available on the last page.

WestBow Press rev. date: 09/02/2015

DEDICATION:

To my wife Lynn

My companion in life and ministry.

My cheerleader and love of my life

CONTENTS

Part Three:
Purpose of Life

INTRODUCTION

Watch Where You're Going

What a thrilling way to start a book, huh? You really want to read this one, don't you? I mean, how many times has someone told you, "Hey, watch where you're going!"? Stay with me; I promise not to sound like a babysitter.

Some of you may be getting your driver's license these days, or maybe you've recently gone through the training to do so. You hear words like these:

> "Keep your eyes on the road."
> "Watch your speed."
> "Don't forget to look in your rearview mirror."
> "Oh, and of course, check the side mirrors too."
> "Both hands on the wheel."

On and on the instructions go. This isn't a driver's instruction manual, but I do want to ask you a question: *do you know where you're going?*

What I mean is, do you recognize the direction of your life these days? This may sound harsh or even cruel, but if you tell me the crowd of friends you hang out with, the music you've been listening to, and the way you respond to the Word of God, I can write the next chapters of your life.

What do I mean by that statement? I mean that if you aren't taking God seriously and you're disobeying His clear-cut commands about choices of friendships and music—if you are ignoring God's Word and not responding with a tender heart of obedience—then I promise you the direction of your life is *not going in the right way!*

In 1 Samuel 2:12–26, we are given a unique glimpse into a Hebrew home. The home consisted of Eli, the father, who was also the high priest of Israel; his two sons, Hophni and Phinehas; and one more boy living with them who was named Samuel. Here were three boys living under the roof of one man. Eli gave them directions every day regarding the proper worship of Jehovah God in the tabernacle. They were taught songs of God, taught how to properly obey God's law, and given responsibilities to perform every day.

However, Hophni and Phinehas didn't want to obey God's directions. They were irreverent, immoral, and indifferent. When their dad confronted them about their choice of friends and direction in life, they didn't listen to him (1 Samuel 2:24). They loved loose women (v. 22). They weren't concerned about the proper way of worshipping God (vv. 12–17) and truthfully didn't even know the Lord personally (v. 12).

Yet, right in the midst of the terrible example of Hophni and Phinehas, there stood a young man, Samuel, who decided to pursue God! Look at verses 21 and 26. Notice that it tells us that Samuel grew in pleasing God. In reality, he grew in his knowledge of the Lord and in obeying Him. People noticed it too, by the way. If you read chapter 3 of 1 Samuel, you will see that people began to recognize the specialness of this young man. He visually showed forth what it meant to be a young man of godly character. How about you? Does anybody recognize that in you?

Samuel pursued the Lord when others didn't. He wanted to know the Lord better. It takes time for any of us to know the Lord better. Remember the apostle Paul said in Philippians 3:10, "That I may know Him …" Wait a minute, hadn't Paul been saved for about thirty years by this time? Yes, but Paul desired to know God even better. Listen to other verses that declare the same truth:

> Ye therefore, beloved, seeing ye know these things before, beware lest ye also, being led away with the error of the wicked, fall from your own steadfastness. But grow in grace, and in the knowledge of our Lord and Savior Jesus Christ. (2 Peter 3:17–18)

> As ye have therefore received Christ Jesus the Lord, so walk ye in Him: rooted and built up in Him, and established in the faith, as ye have been taught, abounding therein with thanksgiving. (Colossians 2:6–7)

> As newborn babes, desire the sincere milk of the Word, that ye may grow thereby. (1 Peter 2:2)

My sister used to tell me, when she was frustrated with me, "Why don't you just grow up?" Do you have an older sister or brother? Has he or she ever told you the same thing? You might agree, that sounds like an unfair request. How does one "grow up"? You can't do it fast. There is no magic button that you can push or pull that helps you to grow up then and there. No, it takes time—a lot of time. But let's face it; we all want to grow up, don't we?

How does one "grow up" in the Lord? It does take time: time walking with Him and getting to know Him, spending time *in* His Word, *listening* to His Word, and, of course, in prayer.

How Are You Doing in These Areas?

If you have never spent much time in the Word of God and you don't really read it much, let me encourage you to start slowly. I'll say more to you about that in a moment, but some of you already try to read God's Word regularly. Maybe it's time to take it up a notch. Maybe you should start tackling some more Bible study. Maybe it's time to start a Bible memorization program. Let me tell you, nothing will help you in the pursuit of God like a regular daily time of being in God's Word. That's how you grow spiritually! By the way, Samuel didn't even have the Bible you have, yet he was learning about his God every day. You can do that!

If you haven't begun regularly reading and meditating on the Bible, let me give a little bit of advice. Start with the Gospel of John. Read one chapter a day as a starter, and just listen to what Jesus does and says throughout the book. After that, read the book of Acts, and then go back to Genesis and start at the beginning. I think you'll see some special truths about God that will revolutionize your life.

For those of you who don't have any friends who are also on the road pursuing the Lord, let me remind you that Samuel was alone too. However, as you turn through the story found for us in the early chapters of 1 Samuel, you'll find that Hophni and Phinehas died an early death, while Samuel went on to be greatly respected of all Israel (1 Samuel 12). You can walk with God too, my young friend. Even alone! Even when no one else wants to, don't lose sight of the end game. Pursuing God pleases God. You won't be sorry.

There were two teenagers sitting in church one Sunday night while their pastor was preaching. The pastor was preaching on the difference between being a carnal believer and a spiritual believer. One young man sat there and began to hear the description of his life—which he was living as a carnal person—and it was not good … at all. He was going in the wrong direction for sure. He looked over at the girl sitting next to him and said, "I'm not going the right way in life; I'm going to give my life to the Lord tonight." The girl became furious and tried to discourage the boy from making such a spiritual decision. She didn't like the pressure it was putting on her; she didn't want to change.

Her anger didn't dissuade the boy. When given the opportunity, he stepped forward and told one of the pastors at the church that he wanted to surrender his life to the Lord that night. The girl left the church that night, never to return. She, in fact, ran away from home later on and wound up with the wrong crowd, became pregnant as a result of her sensual lifestyle, and eventually got arrested because of her participation in stealing a vehicle.

The boy who gave his life to the Lord that night certainly didn't become perfect, but he did attempt to continue in his walk with the Lord. In time, he sensed that God wanted him to preach the Word of God, especially to teenagers. He has given his adult years to trying to help many teenagers. I know this story well, because, you see—the boy was me.

Teenager, start pursuing God today with a regular time in the Word of God. You'll never be sorry. In fact, you'll be forever grateful. Be a Samuel!

Part One:

Pursuing God

Pursuing God

CHAPTER 1
You Are Valuable

I had just pulled into the parking lot of my bank. I needed to hurry inside to take care of some financial transactions before I left town on a ministry trip. That's when I heard it—the advertisement—on the radio.

I had been casually listening to the news when evidently the station had taken a break for some public service announcements and advertisements. A teenage girl's voice came on with an obvious amount of tender emotion. She began by saying she had never taken any drugs, had any liquor, or even smoked a cigarette. She was, it seemed, a fine girl in many ways. However, she went on to say her boyfriend had AIDS. She'd recently found out he had the incurable disease because, well—she had just discovered she had it too.

I couldn't move from the driver's seat of my car. I turned off the engine and thereby the radio. I sat in stunned silence for a few moments. Her voice was powerfully effective. Okay, maybe she was just an actress, but I was genuinely moved. It was probably an advertisement for some program to teach young people about safe sex and that sort of thing. The girl was probably just trying to sell the public on needed education and the necessary funds to carry out such a program, but I couldn't help but wonder: how many teenagers are actually in her predicament, in her condition? How many teenagers have other battles of sorrow in their lives? How many are struggling with thoughts of suicide, problems in their relationship with parents, problems with peer pressure, problems with knowing why they are here on earth? Hurts, sorrows, disappointments, loneliness, wounded spirits, confusion?

It was that day I decided to write this book.

Teenager, let me be honest with you. You don't need to be educated about "safe sex." There's nothing dangerous about it—within its proper place and boundaries. I will say more about that subject later on in the book, but let me simply say this for now: what you desperately need to realize is the importance of living pure and saving yourself for the one person God has in store for you to be your life's mate! I plead with you to commit yourself to live a pure life from this moment on. If you have never committed yourself to the Lord Jesus Christ and to the pure life He desires for you to enjoy, why not do so today?

I know, it may seem that you'll lose out and have no relationship with a boy or with a girl unless you give yourself to sensual pleasure. You've got to understand something: God has a better plan for you. You need to realize this. There's a special day when He will reveal the very person you are to live the rest of your life with and to enjoy fully.

Yet maybe you've already fallen into some level of immorality, or possibly you have no relationship with Christ. *Please keep reading!*

Perhaps you've already faced the trauma of extreme guilt. You may be feeling as if you are worthless trash. I've had far too many teenagers reveal to me the various ways they've tried to take their life because of the guilt they were enduring.

Without a doubt, Satan has done all he can to destroy the fabric of joy and purpose in every person's life. He wants to destroy and eliminate any relationship or fellowship with God. He proved his goal is to dethrone God, but he failed at that; therefore, after being removed from heaven, the devil has spent the rest of his days attempting to destroy God's creation—you and me. He subtly tells you to enjoy anything and everything your flesh wants to do by saying that it is no problem to get involved with such activities. Then after we commit acts of various types of sinful behavior, he screams in our heads—"You're worthless; God can't love you; you're a loser; you're a lousy person."

My young friend, you're not a loser. You are not worthless. You were of such value that Jesus gave His life for you by paying the sin debt you could not pay yourself.

Although I cannot tell you that what you've done is not wrong and sinful, I can inform you of a loving and forgiving God Who desires to help you pick up the pieces and become an overcoming Christian from this day forward. Great news—great news—great news—you can be forgiven! And if you have already pleaded with your God for forgiveness, it is over and done.

The Bible tells us, in 2 Samuel 11, of a time in a king's life when he experienced genuine failure. Not only had he been guilty of committing adultery and murder; he also attempted to ignore the guilt in his heart for well over a year. He had been out of touch with God, guilt-ridden and emotionally disturbed for many months. He wrote about his feelings and sorrow in Psalm 32 as well as Psalm 51. He expressed physical torment, emotional emptiness, and the loss of joy from his life. His body was wracked with severe pain; his rest had been taken from him; and the daily joy of living had long departed.

I wish you would take the time to read Psalm 32 and hear what this man has to say. He actually starts out, if I may paraphrase, by declaring, "Oh, the blessedness of sins forgiven …" He is literally expressing the extreme freedom and peace that came over him after his sins were forgiven by God. You can have your childlike joy once again too, teenager!

You are valuable to God! Yes, you are! Quickly, come to Him today, and seek His forgiveness if you haven't done so yet. Then, once that is settled, do not be guilty of believing you are unimportant and worthless. Trust Him in this hour of decision; lean on the certainty of His Word, the Bible. He lovingly waits for you right now. Express to Him your dependence on His love and forgiveness.

I just wonder: there's probably a parent, a pastor, a youth leader, a godly friend who is praying for you these days and is looking forward to seeing that joy expressed in your countenance once again. If you know who that person is, why not share with them what the Lord has given you today?

God isn't through with you; He's just getting started. Keep reading along in this book, and recognize what kind of heart you ought to have for the Lord and what He has in store for you. You are valuable to Him!

Pursuing God

CHAPTER 2
Living in the Shade

I am not a meteorologist, but I'm fairly certain that it gets hotter in Dallas, Texas, than it does in other parts of the United States where I have lived. I recently took a run in the sun (better stated: a jog from the neighborhood dogs) while in the Dallas area. I couldn't believe how many times I had to stop to catch my breath and recover from the heat. I love to run, and I don't usually mind running in the heat of the day, yet this day was much different. I found myself looking for those spots along the path that were shaded by the overhanging limbs of someone's tree. If the shadow covered a small portion of the road, I would stop and pace back and forth there in the shade. The temperature drop was sufficient for me to enjoy a small time of recuperation before heading back out into the sun. I kept telling myself that it didn't matter that I was stopping, just so long as I was getting in some exercise. Then it hit me, that verse, that song, the message the Lord had tried to give me so many times before.

The verses were found in Psalm 121 which states (vv. 5–8),

> The LORD is thy keeper: the LORD is thy shade upon thy right hand.
> The sun shall not smite thee by day, nor the moon by night.
> The LORD shall preserve thee from all evil: he shall preserve thy soul.
> The LORD shall preserve thy going out and thy coming in from this time forth, and even for evermore.

I remembered how often I had told teenagers that the Lord truly cared for them when they were in the midst of a deep disappointing situation. Maybe a relationship had changed at home, or some other setback caused them to think they couldn't go on. Even though their difficulty seemed "humongous" to them; I would sit and think, "They don't really know what problems are!" Yet I went ahead and told many a teenager, "The Lord is your shade."

(Hey, maybe you're a youth leader or even a parent of a teenager. Let me remind you of what you've told many teenagers—The Lord is your "shade" also. Think about it! Doesn't it get miserably hot from time to time in your life? I know it does. I've heard some of you complain about how things are going. Upset about the lack of faithfulness on the part of your youth group, the bad attitudes of certain "leaders" in the group; and on and on go the complaints. Some of you struggle to make ends meet and have had to spend extra hours working a secular job while trying to be the part-time youth pastor [putting in forty hours a week], battling all kinds of discouragement. The truth is, some of you have forgotten how to enjoy life to its fullest.)

The "heat" is on somehow, some way in your life today. Or maybe it will come before the day is over. Maybe you've been in the midst of trouble and sorrow lately that have caused you to lose a little lilt in your step. What do you need? Why has this happened?

Maybe the Lord is calling you to the Shade, to Himself!

Shade gives comfort, refreshment, solace. Rest. My good friend, I have often found that I enjoy the shade a lot more whenever I am under the duress of the heat. There always seems to be more heat than shade too. So what's the point? The point is simply this: along the daily path of your life, there will always be heat, sometimes more extreme than you can handle. In fact, there will be times when you may think you can't make it any longer. You will have thoughts of running away from it all or even ending it all. What you need at a time like that is shade. You need to run to the Lord!

Why do you think He has said, "Come unto me, all ye that labour and are heavy laden, and I will give you rest"? He is calling you to the shade. His comfort and refreshment await you. When you're scared, when you're bothered, when you're worried, when you're angry, when you're alone, when you're lost in the maze of decisions facing you—run to the shade, run to the Lord. What a privilege, what a blessed truth.

You may be riding in a car right now and you sense the need to talk to your Lord and receive His shade. Maybe you will be sitting in school, with people all around you but still filled with loneliness, when you "run to the shade." Anytime, anywhere, you can find the solace of His shade.

It was an extreme night of loneliness for me. I was sixteen and alone, very alone. I sat and lay down on the living room couch when it happened. I began to cry. I couldn't find anyone to talk to, by phone or even face to face. I felt unneeded and lost in the web of confusion surrounding my future. *What am I going to do with my life, where am I headed?* I decided to read that book I hadn't read for some time, my Bible.

I found myself reading the Psalms with almost a feeling of guilt because it had been so long since I last read the Word of God. Have you ever tried reading and praying at the same time? "Lord, I really am sorry I haven't talked to you lately. I really do want to read your Word. Please be patient with me. Please don't be angry with me." It can be done, but it's hard in the comprehension department.

Fortunately, the Lord stopped my words long enough and caused me to see through the tears to read Psalm 30:5. Have you read it lately? Do you know that verse?

> For his anger endureth but a moment; in his favour is life: weeping may endure for a night, but joy cometh in the morning.

God entered my house, sat down on the edge of my couch, and gave me what I needed. *Shade!* I've told a lot of teenagers about that night; now I'm telling you.

I've been running to those shady spots ever since. Every morning, I go to the reservoir of His Word and find refreshment, comfort, solace, *shade!* I want you to do the same. Stop trying to find it in a new church, a new car, a new friend, a new direction. The desire of my heart is to direct you to the Shade, to the Lord. He and He alone gives you the shade for those times when you have to run in the blazing sun of life. Even for those of you who haven't had any heat lately, you might sometime soon. I guarantee you, He knows what you need. Go to Him, run to Him—now. Wow, it is so good in this shade.

CHAPTER 3

You're Being Lied To

Have you ever caught someone lying to you? It is a pretty miserable feeling, isn't it? In fact, it feels like you've been abused or certainly as if you aren't cared for. I mean, the person lied to you; how can he say he really cares for you, or is a friend?

Well, let me put it like this: have you ever been lied to by someone who thought they were telling you the truth? In other words, what they said made sense to them, but when the truth came out later, it was obvious they had lied! I guess from a technically rigid standpoint they weren't really lying, simply because they didn't know they were.

Case in point: years ago a friend of mine told me I would enjoy riding a particularly strange-looking ride at a theme park. Now, give me anything that goes fast, turns in quick dramatic ways, goes up, down, sideways, backward, and forward, and I'm with you for that kind of ride. However, please keep me off anything that just goes in a round and round and round manner. My body and head doesn't mix well with rides that simply go in fast circles.

I get dizzy, sick to my stomach, and—you don't want to know the rest.

Well, my teenage friend got me to ride this mysterious ride that only looked like a building to me. We walked into a round room, were told to back up to the wall and then it started. The entire room began to turn. It got faster and faster until we were all stuck to the wall. The G force drove us up against the wall until we couldn't pull away. Then they dropped the floor out from under us. Sounds fun? Not really. When they finally turned the ride off, several of us fell to the floor, and then I spent the rest of my day watching the world spin wildly out of control.

My friend kept telling me I would really enjoy this ride. He thought he was telling the truth, but actually, I hated the ride. It made me sick. I felt lied to.

I know someone who lies to us every day. It is his modus operandi. It is his design to lie. He's real good at it, because he's been at it since the beginning of mankind. He has a plan, a purpose and a passion to ruin your life and mine. I speak, of course, of Satan. By the way, when he speaks, he isn't surprised to find out that he has told a lie. It is his plan.

When Jesus was here on earth, He spoke to the religious liars and confused people of that day and said this:

> Ye are of your father the devil, and the lusts of your father ye will do. He was a murderer from the beginning, and abode not in the truth, because there is no truth in him. When he speaketh a lie, he speaketh of his own: for he is a liar, and the father of it. (John 8:44)

Did you catch what Jesus said about the devil? He declared that Satan's motive is to destroy (murder), and his method is deceit (lying). Satan has been in the destroying business from the time of his first conversation with Eve and Adam.

Satan lies about a lot of things. He lies about the importance of money, about matters of purity, about morals, about what makes a person happy. However, his biggest lie is about the biggest Subject, and the biggest Subject is God. He lies to you, teenager, about God. If he can get you to believe a lie about God, he's got you.

You tell me your view of God, and I'll tell you what kind of college you will choose to go to, who you will date and marry, places of entertainment you will frequent—in fact, your view of God will affect not only what you do but what you become.

Satan has no new tricks: he wants to destroy your future marriage, your ministry, your morals, and your mind. He wants to capture the direction of your life. The very last thing he wants to see you do is to *pursue God.* Therefore he lies about God.

Remember the conversation Satan had with Eve in the Garden of Eden? You'll find it in Genesis 3. Listen to his words of deception once again:

> Now the serpent was more subtil than any beast of the field which the LORD God had made. And he said unto the woman, Yea, hath God said, Ye shall not eat of every tree of the garden? (Genesis 3:1)

In that very question, he was attempting to get Eve to question God's goodness to her and Adam. The devil wants all of us to wonder if God is a mean God, attempting to keep things of joy and delight from us. Hear him again ask the question, "Hath God said, ye shall not eat of every tree of the garden?" You can almost see the devil pointing to the Tree of Knowledge of Good and Evil, saying, "Look at how much fun it would be to eat off of the tree. This God you are following is trying to keep fun, laughter, and real joy away from you. If I were you, I'd stop listening to God and enjoy some real living for a change."

He went on to talk with Adam and Eve and encouraged them to believe that they could live *independently* from God. Satan said,

> And the serpent said unto the woman, Ye shall not surely die: For God doth know that in the day ye eat thereof, then your eyes shall be opened, and ye shall be as gods, knowing good and evil. (Genesis 3:4–5)

Hear the words of the devil when he said, "Ye shall not surely die." In other words, Satan was saying, "Go ahead and eat the fruit of the tree. God is trying to keep you from having fun and hold you down. God is mean, and this is your chance to be free of God. Just follow your own desires, and you'll be free; in fact, you'll be as gods."

Teenager, Satan wants you to believe the same lies about your God. He wants you to think that God is mean, that He is keeping things away from you that are fun, that you'll be miserable if you follow Him completely, that God is a killjoy. The devil wants you to think that you'll be miserable if you listen to sermons from God's Word, if you study it for yourself, and if you make your life available to Him. Satan wants you to believe that if you'll just "free" yourself of listening to the Bible, then you'll be truly free. Nothing could be further from the truth!

Can I get you to remember what the Word of God says about our dear Lord? Listen to these two verses in the Psalms.

> Delight thyself also in the LORD: and He shall give thee the desires of thine heart. (Psalm 37:4)
>
> For the LORD God is a sun and shield: the LORD will give grace and glory: no good thing will He withhold from them that walk uprightly. (Psalm 84:11)

Do those two verses sound like God is a mean God? Does it appear that He is trying to keep a full, rich, rewarding life away from those who follow Him? If you're honest, you know that isn't true.

Plainly speaking, *Satan is a liar! God tells the truth!*

Eve should have said, "Look at everything my God has given to us. My God is more than good to us. He is gracious beyond our understanding, and I get to walk with Him every day and listen to Him speak to me and reveal truth to me. Oh don't tell me that my God is mean. He has been more than good to me. Don't make me look at *one tree* and tell me that God is mean. It just gives me a way to show Him how much I love Him by obeying Him and not eating of the fruit from its limbs."

What tree are you looking at these days? What are you afraid that God is keeping from you to enjoy? Are you fearful that the Lord is going to keep you from enjoying life to its fullest; that you might never get married; that you might have to stop enjoying things you like, such as sports, friends, activities?

> But I fear, lest by any means, as the serpent beguiled Eve through his subtilty, so your minds should be corrupted from the simplicity that is in Christ. (2 Corinthians 11:3)

When I was a teenager I struggled with some of the same thoughts and fears you are possibly going through right now. I was afraid that if I gave God the complete control of my life and its future direction, if I surrendered to Him totally, I would probably be a real loser! I feared that I wouldn't play sports ever again. I loved to play sports and wanted to continue to be involved throughout my school years. I could just see it happening: Here I would be surrendering everything to the Lord, and *wham!*—there go the sports, the games, the activities, all of it! I could see myself never playing another game; I would probably wind up sitting around reading books or something (by the way, I'd love to have more time to sit and read books these days, but back then—well?).

You know what happened? I finally surrendered and gave over the control of my life to the Lord, no matter what! The Lord poured out His blessings. He didn't take away my desires; He allowed the fulfillment of them. I played sports throughout high school, throughout college, and then I became a youth pastor and played every game known to humanity, I think! The Lord gave me a hundredfold of my desires.

The same thing was true about my friends too. I feared I would lose all my friends if I put the Lord in first place. Instead of losing, He gave me a superabundance of friends. I can't even keep in touch with all of my friends today.

I was afraid I would never get married, for who would want to marry some guy that was totally committed to Jesus Christ? Wow, was I ever wrong about that! I got the best wife in the whole world. She is my best friend, and we have had a blast going through life together. She is absolutely beautiful and the joy of my life!

No, teenager, you've got your thoughts all messed up about the Lord. He isn't a mean, killjoy, saddened God. He delights in His child who is completely yielded to Him. He gives you "the desires of your heart." Put Him to the test, and you'll see the same thing for you is true.

What are you afraid of when it comes to pursuing the Lord? Are you fearful that you are going to be tied down and never be free, miserably going through life with no real lasting joy or fun?

I know the world around you and its availability of pleasures, possessions, and popularity look so inviting that it seems crazy not to pursue them. Being a Christian who walks with God every day and attempts to know Christ better may even appear boring and miserable to you. Can I tell you something? Satan is lying to you! The most miserable person on the planet is the person who knows Jesus Christ as Savior but doesn't seek to know Him better by pursuing Him. You will never be sorry for following the Lord.

> At thy right hand there are pleasures for evermore.
> (Psalm 16:11)

When Adam and Eve sinned in the Garden of Eden, they tried to hide from God. It didn't work. It won't work for you either. God came looking for Adam and Eve. He is looking for you too. He comes to you now and desires an intimate, intense, intentional walk with you. Will you pursue Him with your whole heart and life? Stop believing the devil's lies; he wants to destroy you. God tells the truth and desires to give you a real reason for living.

> I am come that they might have life, and that they might have it more abundantly. (John 10:10)

CHAPTER 4

Keeping Your Fire

So often I hear about teenagers who are discouraged because they "can't keep their decisions they made for Christ." Of course, youth pastors and youth workers get discouraged also because of the seeming lack of commitment on the part of the young people they are working with. Is there no hope for this problem? How come it seems that some young people "stay by the stuff" while others seem to "die on the vine"?

It goes something like this: The youth group comes home from summer camp where so many teenagers gave their lives to the Lord. Several young men came clean about some sin in their lives and became the "spiritual leaders" on the way home from camp. They even stood up at the front of the bus and led a three-hour singspiration. Everyone, especially the girls, were excited about the real changes they were seeing in so many lives. There was even one girl who wouldn't make a decision for Christ while at camp but, on the way home, couldn't take the pressure anymore and got right with God while talking with a youth leader's wife.

Then on Sunday, there was a special testimony service where all the teenagers had the privilege of standing up in front of the entire church family declaring their allegiance to the Lord. They continually asked for prayer because they understood it wouldn't be easy since they returned home.

Then it happened; the bottom fell out from under them. It just doesn't seem like the singing is the same in youth group meetings. Some boy gets a job and can't make it to all the youth meetings, activities, etc. One by one, others begin to drop out of the group also. A few girls get so discouraged about those guys who "evidently didn't mean it when they got right with God" that they decide not to be so fired up about spiritual things either. Two or three months pass, and it seems like summer camp was a distant memory. How did it happen? Why did it happen? Everyone seemed to mean their decision for the Lord. Those tears at the final camp service were real, weren't they? Why can't anyone stay right with God these days?

Sound familiar? Probably so. I don't know of too many youth groups that haven't experienced some sort of disappointments such as the made-up one you just read about. Can I help you? Please listen to my heart for a few moments of your time, and allow the Lord to work in your heart.

Even though young people stood up and asked others to pray for them because they knew it was going to be hard, trying to stay "on fire for God," they still fell away. Why? I believe part of the problem is that they somehow thought their *feelings* would override the daily onslaught from the wicked one, Satan. They were riding so high on emotion after a week of camp, or the revival meeting or something like it, that they assumed they would always feel this good. Young person, remember this: feelings come and go. You don't live the Christian life or stay consistent for Christ based on *feelings*. It is a battle—daily—moment by moment—continually. You'd better get prepared for it.

The apostle Paul was concerned about his good ministry friend, Timothy, when he wrote him the second letter. Remember those words in 2 Timothy 1? In fact if you would read chapters 1 and 2 right now, it would work in your favor as we continue talking about this matter. Please do it. It will only take a few extra minutes, and then I want to show you several items of great importance.

Now that you've read 2 Timothy 1 and 2, did you notice several things regarding the battle we're in? He said to Timothy,

> Thou therefore, my son, be strong in the grace that is in Christ Jesus.
>
> ....
>
> Thou therefore endure hardness, as a good soldier of Jesus Christ.

You see, you are in a battle, and you have to maintain your spiritual strength if you plan to stay "on fire."

Now look back at 2 Timothy 1:6, which says, "Wherefore I put thee in remembrance that thou stir up the gift of God …" This means, to fan into a flame the original fire that God produced in your heart and life. In other words, the Lord doesn't want you to lose fire or fervency either.

There's another great truth I saw while reading through these two chapters. It seemed as though there were others who were turning aside from the truth of God and from the Christian faith. Paul was telling Timothy to march on regardless of what others chose to do.

So here's what I'm trying to say to you: You can't make others, your friends, do right or stay right with God, but *you have a choice!* What are you planning to do? Let me give you a few things to remember in order to keep the fires fanned into a mighty flame!

Get a Fresh Purpose

By this I mean, determine what it is you want to do with your life. Do you want to continually live for self and your flesh, or do you hunger to please God with your life? Paul told Timothy not to be ashamed of the gospel or of the holy calling which he had received from the Lord. He actually encouraged Timothy to participate in the hardships of the battle.

Then there was the verse in chapter 2 where Paul told Timothy to invest time in others ("faithful men") and teach them how to serve the Lord. Teenager, do you have a ministry? I'm not asking you if you play an instrument in the church services, work in the nursery, help clean up after vacation Bible school. I mean this: do you have a ministry with someone else who desires to grow in their walk with the Lord? I'm telling you the truth, if you will give yourself to the development of others spiritually, you'll be amazed at what it does for your own "fire." You will sense the great need to stay on fire for God because you are trying to help others to do the same. Find someone who is a young Christian, or better still, ask the Lord to give you someone to witness to and then disciple yourself. Wow, what a great and glorious privilege that would be. This is the fresh purpose you need!

A Fresh Perusal of Scriptures

What does *peruse* mean? It means to examine thoroughly; to inspect and scrutinize over. If you want to know why the overwhelming majority of young people don't stay "on fire" for the Lord after a recent decision for Him, this is the reason! In fact, I'm wondering if this isn't the case 100 percent of the time.

If you aren't in the Word of God on a daily basis, with a desire to hear from your Lord, I guarantee that it won't be any time before you will be away from Him. You must be in the Word of God every day! Spiritual stagnation is the only thing waiting for you if you aren't feeding on the Bible for daily sustenance and strengthening. You just can't make it! Second Timothy 1:13 tells us to hang onto the healthy teaching of God's Word.

> His word was in mine heart as a burning fire shut up in my bones. (Jeremiah 20:9)
>
> This second epistle, beloved, I now write unto you; in both which I stir up your pure minds by way of remembrance: That ye may be mindful of the words which were spoken before by the holy prophets, and of the commandment of us the apostles of the Lord and Saviour: (2 Peter 3:1–2)
>
> And they said one to another, Did not our heart burn within us, while he talked with us by the way, and while he opened to us the scriptures? (Luke 24:32)

I have never known a teenager to "stick" with his/her decision for Christ who wasn't in the Bible every day. You won't make it either, I promise! If you haven't been reading God's Word, ask for forgiveness, and commit yourself to a reading program once again. Get back in the battle, soldier. We need you!

CHAPTER 5

Are You Troubled?

Do you remember the time a friend told you about a conversation she had with someone and you thought, "Oh I wish I could have seen her face when you said that!"? Or maybe you heard about a special gift someone was going to receive, and you got to see their surprised, somewhat out of control expression upon learning or seeing the gift.

Here's another question for you: Is there a Bible event that you wish you could have seen "live"? You wish you could have been there when it happened? For me there are many stories I wish I could have been the old "fly on the wall," taking in everybody's expression.

Here's one event I definitely would have loved seeing. It's the time when Joseph revealed himself to his brothers in Genesis 45. He told them that he was their brother they had sold off into slavery some twenty-two years before. I love this story! Joseph said in Genesis 45:3, "I am Joseph; doth my father yet live?" Here's the most powerful man in the most powerful kingdom facing those men who had hated him years ago and saying, "I'm your brother."

In previous conversations with Joseph, they had no knowledge it was him because he had come across as a gruff, difficult Egyptian. In essence he was saying, "I'm the one you hatefully stuffed down into a pit and then yanked out in order to make a few pieces of silver off the sale of my life to the traders who were headed down here to Egypt, where I became a slave and prisoner, but now I'm powerful enough to have your heads chopped off. Good to see you, boys; how's Dad?"

I would have loved to see the expression on those guys' faces, wouldn't you? When Joseph asked about his Dad the rest of verse 3 declares, "and his brethren could not answer him, for they were troubled at his presence." No kidding! You and I would have been troubled too!

Teenager, is something troubling you today? Have you been troubled lately? What is it that is eating away at you?

Throughout the Bible the word *troubled* means "agitated; made turbulent, stirred up." It is the idea of an inner turmoil that takes your breath away, causing you to gasp!

People are troubled over all kinds of things—events, statements made to them or about them, or just plain unanswered questions in their lives. Teenagers get troubled when they think they don't have a friend in the world. Some become convinced they aren't very good at anything, like sports, music, or school. Then there are those times when a person becomes troubled because they have become convinced that God doesn't love or care for them.

What ridiculous, unbiblical thinking! I'm serious! Put your feelings on hold for a moment and hear me out: *Jesus never enjoyed seeing a troubled heart!* All the time, Jesus was comforting people when He walked on this earth. Remember the time in Matthew

14 when the Lord Jesus came walking on the turbulent waters toward the disciples? The Bible says they were troubled and cried out in fear. Yet verse 27 tells us that Jesus "straightway" spoke to bring calmness to their hearts and souls. The word *straightway* means "immediately." Jesus didn't let them sit in fear, shrieking out of control, and then try to calm them. No, He immediately spoke peace to their souls.

In Luke 24, the resurrected Jesus appeared with the disciples while they gathered together discussing the possibility of His resurrection. Upon seeing Jesus, "they were terrified and affrighted." Again He immediately put a stop to that by saying, "Why are ye troubled? And why do thoughts arise in your hearts?"

I'm telling you, Jesus made it His business to go around seeking to calm troubled hearts. He didn't enjoy seeing His followers troubled then, nor does He enjoy it now—in you.

One more example on this truth: In John 11 Jesus walked into the cemetery where His friend Lazarus was buried. Jesus was about to raise Lazarus from the dead, and He knew it. Yet as He observed the hurting hearts, the groaning and mourning, He wept. In fact, John 11:33 tells us that He joined them in their *troubled state.*

Look, what am I trying to state here? Simply this: Anything that now troubles you, or ever has, is something the Lord wants to take away from you—right now!

Some of you have the idea that He doesn't care about your burden; that your concerns are too unimportant to Him. That is offensive in the eyes of God. Don't make your God a "little god." He isn't too busy to hear your troubled heart! His hands aren't so tied up with bigger problems elsewhere that He can't find the time to address your heartache.

If you don't believe me, why not take this test? Right now after you read this chapter, turn to Psalm 46 and read it. Read it carefully and slowly. Ask the Lord to reveal Himself to you as you do so. Then do the same thing with Psalm 91. After sitting down with the Lord in those two texts and allowing Him to hold you, speak as a child to your Father. Tell Him of your troubled heart. He already knows about it, but go ahead and tell Him what is troubling you. Let Him know you want to do whatever pleases Him, and then close by thanking Him for listening to your troubled heart.

You know what you'll be doing by this practice? The same thing revealed in the contrast between Martha and Mary in Luke 10. Martha was frantic, i.e., troubled about doing something for her Master. Mary, however, simply sat at His feet to hear Him, to *be with* Him. Jesus turned to the troubled Martha (vv. 41–42) and said, "Martha, Martha, thou art careful and troubled about many things. But one thing is needful: and Mary hath chosen that good part, which shall not be taken away from her."

Okay, I'm gonna hush and let you go sit at Jesus' feet. He calms the troubled sea, the troubled mind, and the troubled heart. Before you do, let me tell you about one particular night when the Lord calmed me.

I had just walked home from a baseball field. It was about a five-mile walk. I can't remember how I was supposed to get home, but I decided to walk. Why? Because of that girl. You see, there had been a girl I liked quite a bit, but she evidently no longer liked me. This seems so petty to me while I tell you about this, but it was big-time when it occurred.

This girl had told me there in the bleachers that she now liked some other guy. This other guy was a better athlete than me, I knew. He was funnier than me, I knew. He was, from her vantage point, better than me in many areas. Well, I had had it with her. I told her I was going to go to the concession stand to buy some fries and a Coke. I walked by the concessions and kept on walking … five miles, all the way home. I'm not sure what I was trying to prove to her, but I just couldn't stay any longer. I was hurting; I was troubled.

Now I know this story may seem silly to you, but if you told me what troubles you today, maybe it would seem equally ridiculous. So just hear me out.

I got home, sweaty from the walk, and still torn up inside. I didn't have anyone to talk to, I thought. Then in the midst of my sorrow, I remembered a friend I hadn't talked to for quite some time—my Lord! Actually, I couldn't call Him "my Lord." Even though I was saved, which made Him my Savior, I wasn't allowing Him to be the Master and King of my life. Really, I had been living too much for myself. In actuality, I had attempted to be the master of my life and had made a mess of things.

So I went to my Bible and to my knees. I told the Lord I was sorry for not being devoted to Him. I needed to hear from Him. I don't know what made me turn to the Psalms, but I did. I read Psalm 20 and kept reading through Psalm 40—twenty-one Psalms in all. I'm telling you, teenager: He comforted me. My heart was calmed. He will do the same for you.

Right now, go let Him calm your troubled soul. Get forgiveness for a life out of tune with Him and "be still and know that He is God."

Pursuing God

CHAPTER 6

Becoming a Champion

It's a thought many guys have had while daydreaming in school. They're in a ball game of some kind against their biggest opponent. It may be basketball, football, baseball, maybe tennis; whatever they enjoy playing. Well anyway, here's their thought: the clock is winding down, and the pressure is on. My team is down in the score, yet at the last moment I throw the winning touchdown pass or shoot the winning basket or hit the home run (maybe even a grand slam) to win the game. I'm telling you that many guys have had that thought enter their mind—probably many times.

Well, let me ratchet up the scene a bit more. Imagine the opponent you're going up against is not the biggest rival in your school, but let's say it's a professional athlete. Yeah, right, I know it's never going to happen, but stay with me. Imagine going up against the biggest name team in whatever sport you would daydream about. There stands the huge team composed of grown men against you, and they are well-oiled machines as athletes.

You probably couldn't get a jump-shot off without them blocking you. You probably couldn't throw a pass to any receiver downfield without them tackling you with such force that several bones would never be the same. If they were pitching to you while you stood in the batter's box, you probably wouldn't even see the baseball sail past you.

What a joke to consider it possible for you to compete against a professional athlete in any sport, right? And it's a bigger joke to think that you could defeat them at their specialty. Now you have a little better idea of what happened the day David defeated Goliath.

Now stay with me, teenager. I know you've heard this story of David your whole life. You've heard it and heard it and heard it so much that it doesn't even have the force of great truth or impact in your thoughts anymore. Maybe it was one of your favorite stories when you were a small kid, but today, it almost seems like a fairy tale. Got news for you, teenager: it actually happened. David, a teenage boy of some fifteen years of age killed a grown man who was trained as a soldier. A giant of a man, that is. Goliath was somewhere between nine foot six inches and twelve feet tall. Scholars have debated how big he was for years. Just realize this—he was a giant of a man. Not only that, he was a professional warrior. David wasn't supposed to defeat him, but he did—soundly! He took his head off his shoulders.

There are things, habits, and areas in your life that seem invincible, I'm sure. There are some areas in your life that are keeping you from having God's very best! There is a temptation that seems larger than any other temptation! It is a giant in your life.

Giants reveal what we really are! Giants seem so intimidating and large that they appear unbeatable. These giant areas of temptation consume you, control you, and defeat you. You want to be a victorious Christian teenager, but you feel defeated by this giant of a problem in your life.

Am I right? I feel certain I am. You see, I've had some fairly serious conversations with teenagers down through the years who felt as if there was no way they could overcome this giant problem of temptation in their life.

Your giant may be immorality of some type or another; it may be idolatry of some sort (an idol being anything that has become bigger than God Himself in your life); it may be insecurity. You have no confidence in yourself to overcome sin and its continual presence in your thoughts and life.

Are you feeling defeated? Do you think there is no way you could ever overcome this giant in your life? How come David was able to defeat Goliath in his day, and you can't do it in your day? Answer: *you can!* The same God that David knew is the same God you can know today!

I find several reasons why David was able to go out there and overcome Goliath with such confidence, but there was one big main reason.

David was a humble, obedient boy at home first of all. He did what his parents told him to do, even after being anointed by the great prophet Samuel and being told that he (David) would be the next king of Israel. Think about it; he could have told his parents to bug off because he was going to be the king someday—but he never did talk that way to his parents. Genuinely, he obeyed them. He faithfully took care of the sheep each day as he was told.

He also was humble when success and victory came his way. Yet, I still find another main reason why David was a winner when confronted with this giant. Would you like to know what it is?

Listen to these words of David, found in 1 Samuel 17:45: "Thou comest to me with a sword, and with a spear, and with a shield: but I come to thee in the name of the LORD of hosts, the God of the armies of Israel, whom thou hast defied."

Then read the next verse:

> This day will the LORD deliver thee into mine hand … that all the earth may know that there is a God in Israel.

Verse 47 continues the heartbeat of this champion young man:

> And all this assembly shall know that the LORD saveth not with sword and spear; for the battle is the LORD's, and He will give you into our hands.

Did you catch it? David went out on the battle field realizing that he was not alone. He faced Goliath *with the Lord!* There's the truth we've got to understand. David knew the Lord personally; intimately; intensely! David knew that God would defeat Goliath. How did he know that? Because David knew the Lord!

Young person, I wish I could look you straight in the eyes and say this: you've got to know the Lord! How well do you really know Him? Are you pursuing a growing knowledge of Him?

I'm not asking you if you go to church, occasionally read your Bible and pray, even sing songs of worship while at church. I'm talking about pursuing God.

It takes time to get to know the Lord. Time spent with Him each day; time spent throughout the day. You've got to schedule a specific time when you shut out all other noises, all other plans, all other voices, all other thoughts and just let the Lord have your complete attention. Open your Bible and ask the Lord to reveal Himself to you. There's no other way to fulfill the journey of getting to know the Lord.

If you asked me to tell you about my wife, I could give you details about her that would include her height, her favorite colors, her favorite meals, the color of her hair, her birth date, etc. But that would only be a bunch of facts. I've got news for you, I know my wife. I can tell you what she is feeling at almost any given moment; I can tell you what makes her feel better, what makes her laugh, what her thoughts are when someone else is speaking, etc. Why is that? Because I've spent a lot of years with my wife—I know her!

For some of you, your knowledge of God is only a bunch of facts: He is omnipotent, omniscient, omnipresent, immutable, etc. But how well do you know the heartbeat of your God? David knew Him! He knew that God would bring victory out on the battlefield against a giant of a man.

David knew the Lord because he spent time with Him every day. You can imagine David out taking care of his sheep and talking to his Lord at the same time. David would pray to Him, sing to Him, write words about Him. If David lived today, he would be tempted to have earphones in his ears listening to some form of music coming from his iPod, or maybe he would have his phone to his ear. Probably he would have some miniature computer out there in the fields, checking various websites or maybe just texting his friends rather than keeping a close eye on the sheep. If David lived today, we would probably have never received the Twenty-Third Psalm. For that matter, most of the Psalms would never have been written because David would have been so distracted with other outside noises. He would not have been able to hear the voice of God. Nor would he have been able to defeat Goliath.

There it is, teenager. You've got to walk with God each day. Pursue Him! You've got to turn off the computer and the TV, get away from the phone, put aside other matters, and let God have your complete attention. Not only that, you need to *pursue* the Lord. Go to Him and ask Him to reveal Himself to you! Tell Him you are tired of being a defeated teenager. You want to start overcoming the giants in your life, and you realize that it is impossible without His presence and power.

I'm praying for you, teenager, that you will become a champion of God while being reminded of a teenage boy many years ago who was a champion in his day. We need some Davids today!

CHAPTER 7

Born to Be Wild

I used to be a camp director in Arizona. I had the privilege of working with some great churches, and in particular, I got to be with a lot of teenagers from all over the southwest section of our great country. We had some great weeks of camp and retreats for people of all ages; I have some great memories of those years. Well, our camp ministry had a Western/cowboy motif about it which included a rodeo every week of summer camp. This was a rodeo for the campers to participate in which included events such as a tug-o'-war, chasing a pig, mounting a horse, sack races, etc. It was great, and the kids loved it.

As we approached our first ever rodeo, our staff spoke to me about the "importance" of having a grand entry into the rodeo arena. This meant they felt we needed someone to bring in the American flag and for the camp director, which was me, to ride into the arena on a horse, lead everyone in the Pledge of Allegiance, and then have prayer. Get the picture: I was to gallop in on a horse. Okay, maybe you need a little help with this scene.

Here I am, a city slicker, supposed to ride/gallop into the rodeo arena with an impressive-looking horse. Well, it was no problem to have an impressive-looking horse, but my galloping had never existed before. I didn't know how to make a horse run as our staff felt I needed it to do. Therefore I needed to practice.

Several days before our first rodeo, I practiced—a lot! I got fairly comfortable with a horse, and I thought everything was going to be great. Then the first rodeo day came; the moment of truth was upon us. It came time for me to enter into the arena on a galloping horse. I was outside the arena; I spoke to the horse (actually I shouted something like "hiyahhhhhh!"), but the horse froze. I mean, there was no movement whatsoever. He was intimidated with all those campers around. The horse was out of his comfort zone and would not move. I kicked, pleaded, hollered, and even tried to find the key to start his ignition; nothing worked. I looked around at the staff, and they all were laughing. I couldn't get the horse to move one inch.

You see, when we were all alone a few days prior, he would run with no problem. However, at that time there were no campers around. Now I was asking him to do something completely out of his boundary of normalcy. Simply stated, he was a rebel!

I wonder if we really understand and recognize true rebellion. We all think rebellion is something others participate in and practice. We picture rebellion always as something like becoming a drunk, a drug addict, a pervert, someone with a repulsive lifestyle. It is usually someone else's music choices, dress choices, language, and entertainment choices that we perceive as being rebellious. We never look at ourselves and consider ourselves as a rebel.

Isaiah was a true prophet who had the task of telling God's people that they were in rebellion. In his very first address to Judah we find Isaiah telling them they were rebels. You see it in chapter 1, verse 2 ("I have nourished and brought up children, and they have rebelled against me") and also in verse 20, where he says: "But if ye refuse and rebel, ye shall be devoured with the sword."

We begin to see God's description of rebellion and then God's prescription for rebellion. It would be wise for us to recognize God's description of rebellion first. It might surprise you what it looks like.

A DEAFENED PEOPLE

Isaiah tells God's people to "hear"; "give ear" to the words of God. Actually he tells them that God has already "spoken," and they weren't listening to Him.

So often we become guilty of not genuinely listening to our Lord when He speaks. Are you guilty of attending church and hearing the messages from your pastor or youth leaders without actually hearing anything specifically for you? Have you been reading your Bible on a regular basis and not really coming away with anything exclusively for you?

Rebellion is first and foremost a problem with our spiritual ears becoming clogged with all the other "noises" of our world. We then become unable to actually *hear* our God speaking to us!

Sometimes we come to the Word of God for information; sometimes we go to it for inspiration. Nothing wrong with either of those motivations for reading the Bible; however, there is a much more crucial reason to read God's Word—transformation! We are to be in the process of being transformed into the image of Jesus Christ.

> For whom He did foreknow, He also did predestinate to be conformed to the image of His Son. (Romans 8:29)

In order to be transformed, we must allow our Lord to clearly speak to us from His Word. We have to be listening to Him and *hear* Him with our hearts!

I think we actually become somewhat spiritually deaf to the Bible because many of us have heard it so often through the years. We've heard the stories, heard the classic passages, heard the teaching and preaching so much that we stop hearing it. How else can you explain people like Samson, Demas, Lot, and others throughout the Bible who became so used to the teachings of God that they evidently stopped listening to it?

A DESENSITIZED PEOPLE

In time, spiritual deafness leads to spiritual desensitization. We get to the point that we don't respond to God anymore. We actually become comfortable with a lukewarm existence with God. Dangerous!

Isaiah tells us in his first chapter that the people of God actually didn't respond to His dealings with them anymore. They were worse than animals. Isaiah states that donkeys and oxen respond to their masters better than we respond to our God. What a condemning analogy.

It is at this point that we notice something very important from the words of Isaiah. He gives us clear answers to our dilemma of inborn rebellion. You see, teenager, there is a little rebel in each one of us. We'd better recognize that we have a tendency to become deaf and desensitized to our God from time to time. Well how do we deal with this inclination toward a rebellious heart?

First of all we are to come to God with *sincere reverence*. What does that mean actually? It means to allow and long for a genuine adoration and worship of God. It will cause sensitivity for the Master's voice in your heart and life. It means that we actually live with the constant awareness of God's presence among us and that we long for it to be so.

I can recall enjoying visits to my grandfather's house when I was a little boy. To go see Granddaddy meant riding a motorcycle in the country, playing in the big tree in the front yard, shooting BB guns, and exploring the country life. As a boy I was only thinking of myself and what I could enjoy by being somewhat near my grandfather's house.

As I got older, however, I began to realize how much fun it was to sit and listen to my granddad talk about his life. I just enjoyed being near him—not what I could do outside, but inside the house near my granddad.

Do you see it? There needs to be the development of awareness of what you glean from being in the presence of your Lord. Don't be guilty of just thinking of all that the Lord will do *for* you if you get around Him; be hungry to simply be *near* Him. Rebellion is treated when we thirst after God.

Secondly, Isaiah tells us to live with *sober repentance*.

> Wash you, make you clean; put away the evil of your doings from before mine eyes; cease to do evil. (Isaiah 1:16)

We have to call sin what it is: transgression against our Lord. If you really want to come clean with God and deal with the penchant for rebellion, you're going to repent. Agree with God that what you've thought, done, or considered is unclean and that you desire to receive forgiveness.

Teenager, have you gotten comfortable with some sinful behavior in your life? Have you excused it and tolerated it? Is the Holy Spirit bringing that particular matter to your mind even right now? Get serious about dealing with it, and tell the Lord you want to be made clean spiritually.

Every spring I look at my yard and I see those annual little "greetings"; they're called weeds. I kill those little ugly guys every year with fertilizer, sprays, and even a professional company that promises to get rid of those pesky little weeds. However, every spring, there they are once again.

Why do they return? Because they're in the soil! I'm convinced there is a hidden world underneath the soil called "weed-dom" (the kingdom of weeds and all their cousins). They wait until I'm not looking and then bounce back up in my front yard, all at the same time (they plan that too: "everybody ready … okay: one, two, three—*grow*"). I throw fertilizer and sprays on them, and I can hear them underneath the soil laughing and saying, "Thanks for the nutrition; this tastes great; we'll be back, mister."

Okay, I'm not really crazy—just disturbed at my front yard of "weed-dom." In the soil of my yard are the elements of weeds and all that produces them.

In the soil of your life and in mine are the elements of sin. They are ever present. You might be moving along quite well, thinking that you're living victoriously and then it happens: the "weed" of your sin nature pops up. It is always there; it always will be there until we get to heaven and receive a new nature.

What do we do? Repent! Faithfully, consistently, sincerely, regularly *repent!* Keep dealing with it by going to your Lord and receiving forgiveness. Thankfully, He is always faithful to forgive us and to cleanse us from our unrighteous behavior. Thankfully, He is a forgiving Lord.

Sometimes it's hard to admit it, but there is a little rebel in every one of us. For further reference, take a look at little children, and watch them fuss over toys with other children. Take a look at adults, and watch how they live their lives. Oh yeah, and take a long, long look at your own life. You were born with a rebel's heart, but there is healing, cleansing, and conquest over it.

Part Two:
Purity of Heart

Purity of Heart

CHAPTER 8
Just a Friend

It started out rather innocently. Four teenage boys walking down a familiar street where three of the boys lived. To the one teenage boy, who was not totally aware of his surroundings, he thought it was a simple fun walk on a cool summer night. It did seem a bit unusual, however, when with each step down the sidewalk, the pace seemed to pick up. After about a hundred yards the four boys were practically running. There seemed to be an air of nervous excitement.

Then everyone stopped when one of the older boys nervously whispered, "There it is!" *It* was a car—an old one. A really, really old car; but a car nonetheless. Before anyone could say much else, all four boys piled into it. The one teenage boy unfamiliar with the territory was somewhat unsettled in his spirit; why the fuss and excitement over such an ugly old car? Yet he didn't say anything for fear of being laughed at.

As the boys continued their drive around the neighborhood, the driver had the unusual habit of turning off the headlights every time he pulled up to an intersection. This prompted the young man (who was a Christian, by the way) to ask, "What's going on? Why do you keep turning off your lights?"

With a quiet giggle, the boy riding shotgun simply said, "It's not his car, and he doesn't even have a license."

It felt as if someone had hit him in the midsection; he could hardly breathe. What was he doing with a bunch of guys in a stolen car? The conversation continued in the car, and he gathered enough to realize that the vehicle belonged to the driver's parents, who evidently were out for the evening and totally unaware of their son's misdeeds.

What would you have done? Would you even be with this group? To be fair, this particular Christian boy had been completely in the dark about these plans to run around in a car, taken without permission, being driven by someone without a driver's license. He thought he was just hanging out with friends having some fun—some innocent fun. Innocent it started, but criminal it became!

Once the car came to a halt at a stop sign, the troubled Christian teenager, in the backseat, opened the back door and simply said, "I'm heading for the house; I'll see you there." The others frantically begged him to get back in the car for fear themselves. They all knew it was wrong to do what they were doing; having someone say he didn't want to be a part of their plans only made it worse. The Christian boy knew he could no longer continue riding in the car. If his friends got caught or not he did not know; he simply knew he had already been "caught" by the Lord. He had discovered the trouble with hanging out with the wrong crowd—it always brings problems eventually. It may start out fun, but it will end disastrously.

One thing has done more to ruin teenagers than practically everything else in the world—*bad friends!* In most cases, it's just the influence of *one* bad friend. *Ungodly friends will hurt you—most of the time, beyond recovery.*

Everyone wants to have friends. In fact we need good friends to help us. To be more specific, we need Godly friends to build us up in our spiritual lives. Young person, if you continually spend time with another teenager or a group of teenagers who are not committed to living for God, you have placed yourself in an environment that will (I repeat, WILL) lead you to do things you never dreamed of doing.

How many teenagers have lost their purity, lost their testimony, became active in shoplifting, started laughing at dirty jokes, begun speaking with vulgar obscenities, entered a pornographic lifestyle, lied to their parents, and forsaken going to church, reading the Bible, and consciously thinking on God? All because of the influence of another ungodly teenager.

How does it happen? Well, let's be honest! You want to have friends—that's a given, and it's natural. Sometimes the easiest friend to get is someone who isn't living for Christ. In an effort to be accepted or even to be popular, a teenager gets drawn slowly into a life of sin, and godly living is left far behind. It could even start with an ungodly association in the church youth group. Sitting in the back of the church auditorium, laughing and talking during the church worship service, ignoring anyone's pleas to listen—it's all a part of the subtle plan.

Amnon (2 Samuel 13:1–12) had a "friend" by the name of Jonadab. That so-called friend led this firstborn son of David to miss the mark of being the next king of Israel, helping bring about disaster in Amnon's life. Jonadab, with crafty words, led Amnon into defilement of lustful sin, taught him how to lie, and indirectly led to his death. Think of it. Here was a young man who should have become Israel's next king, but he never made it. Why? One friend!

You could miss the right marriage, the right vocation, the right college, the right future! How? One friend.

Stop right now, teenager. Evaluate your friendships. Are your friends really helping you grow spiritually? How about this hard question—Is the person you're dating helping you spiritually? Are you a better Christian because of the friends you have, the people you spend time with, your closest companions?

Your fear is genuine, I know. If you stop hanging out with those particular friends, you fear you'll have no friends at all. Nothing could be further from the truth. Let me give you a bit more advice:

1. Don't go looking for friends. Let the Lord bring them to you. God will honor your commitment to godly living and your desire to please Him. Be patient; the right set of friends will be yours in time. Even Adam, the first man in the Garden of Eden, was alone for a while. He focused on his relationship and fellowship with God. In time, the Lord brought a great friend, Eve, to Adam.
2. Continue in your march to please the Lord. Live for God, walk with God, and keep a short account with God. Stay

on the right path! Those who are doing the same and want to do the same will eventually come your way, and together you will have lots in common.

3. Resolve, decide, *determine* to never date someone who is unsaved or not desiring to live a godly life!

Maybe it's time for you to "get out of the car" with those friends too. If they're not helping you draw closer to your Lord, then they are hindering you.

CHAPTER 9

The Stiff-Arm

It's the kind of football play that gets real fans out of their seats. Sometimes you even try to help the runner get a few more yards down the field. It is when your team needs those desperately important yards and the running back on your team heads upfield. He firmly hangs onto the football in one arm while balancing himself with the other.

Then an opposing player comes at him full force. That's when the ball-carrier, who has been properly trained in the skill of running, does it: he stiff-arms the guy! You've seen it done. He takes his non-ball-carrying arm and drives his hand into the chest or headgear of the opponent, keeping him an arm's distance away. He stiffens his arm, holding off the foe.

That's what you do to your opponent—someone who is trying to hurt you, to slow you, to stop your movement forward. My question to you, teenager, is this: who are you stiff-arming? I have spent many years trying to help young people keep the real opponent, Satan, away from them. Sadly, in fact regrettably, too few young people stiff-arm him. Instead, I've seen many teenagers actually keep the Lord Himself at arm's length!

I've seen these young people by the scores. They give an appearance they are following the Lord, when in truth they are keeping Him distant—close enough to pray to when things are desperate; but not fully embraced. No, there's no full embrace of all that the Lord is, all that He wants for them, all that He commands.

Instead, there's the stiff-arm: keeping the Lord just out of reach. These teenagers are in the arena, looking the part of a good and godly Christian, but they're not committed to Him. They appear to be close, but they're not intimate with Him. They want to recall their previous decisions of surrender without seeming weird to the world around them. They are following, at a distance—"afar off."

The disciple Peter did this when Jesus was being taken to the trial before Caiphas and the Sanhedrin (Matthew 26:57–75). Peter was following "afar off." He was shy about his commitment to Jesus Christ because he was afraid.

Are you afraid?

Afraid of being made fun of?

Afraid of being hurt by others and losing their acceptance?

Afraid of having no more fun?

Afraid of being considered odd and weird?

Are you following Jesus "afar off"? Are you keeping the Lord at an arm's distance?

When you live like this, teenager, you will have some of these kinds of characteristics:

1. You have a daily quiet time with the Lord, but the motivation is more out of routine or fear of "getting in trouble" with God. There's nothing sweetly intimate about it.
2. You sing in church, but not too fervently or heartily.
3. You listen to preaching and teaching of God's Word, but only to what won't bring conviction or deal with a fully surrendered life.
4. You may have a prayer request when asked, but there is refusal to repent of your own sinfulness.
5. You enjoy talking to others, but never about the Lord.
6. You are passionate about other events in your life, but not about knowing the Lord in a deeper manner.

Like Peter, such believers follow afar off.

Teenager, if you're finding your heart strangely sensing this in your own life, let's take a closer look at this matter and make several observations. These are truths about any believer who stiff-arms God.

1. You'll Eventually Find Yourself with the Wrong Crowd.

In fact, you may have already taken this step. In many cases, teenagers continue stiff-arming their Lord because they want the acceptance of this crowd. Peter found the wrong crowd at a stranger's fire. It was there that Peter denied even knowing Jesus Christ. This crowd who doesn't know the Lord, who will crucify the Lord, never makes for good friends. That will become your crowd if you stiff-arm the Lord.

2. You Will Tumble Into Further Sin and Sorrow, Rather Quickly!

I wish I didn't know as many stories as I do of teenagers who followed the Lord from a distance. They now have experienced many other tragedies as a result of living at a distance from their Lord Jesus. Some fall into immorality, some into crime, and some into a mental breakdown. It happened because they kept the Lord at an arm's distance. Peter eventually cursed and carried himself as anything but a true disciple and follower of Christ (Matthew 26:69–75). You will do the same if you continue on this path.

3. Those Who Stiff-Arm the Lord Are Often Those Who Have Known Special Privileges or Blessings.

Think of all that Peter has seen and experienced; yet here he is denying the Lord. Peter doesn't even look like a follower of His. He has been privileged to see the Lord work in many wonderful ways: feeding the hungry, healing the sick, walking on water, calming the storms, and much, much more.

But wait, you've been privileged too! Think about it. You've seen answers to prayer; you have the privileges of being a Christian; some of you have Christian parents; most of you have a good solid Bible teaching church to attend; you have many good friends; you own a Bible; you have daily food and clothing; and much, much more!

Some of you sing in youth choirs, participate on Bible Quiz teams; go on trips with your youth group and youth leaders. Some of you have even been used of the Lord to lead other people to Christ.

You've been blessed greatly! Yet today you are keeping the Lord Jesus at an arm's distance; not willing to fully embrace Him.

4. Many Times Your Condition Is Revealed in Your Speech.

Peter spoke in angry tones; he even cursed. Have you started to use angry talk? Are you an angry person? How often do you lose your temper? Once a week? Once a day? Once an hour? More frequently than what you used to?

Maybe this temper problem of yours occurs as a result of you ignoring the fact that you are following the Lord, afar off.

But wait: I've got great news. Peter didn't stay this way. He soon saw His Lord again (Luke 22:61) and then he saw what he had done to Jesus. Peter saw his cold, sinful condition, and the Bible says that he "went out, and wept bitterly." I know that may not sound like good news, but this is the start of a changed man. Peter repented. He was broken. Are you? Do you ever weep over the direction of your life? Does it burden you that you've been stiff-arming the Lord instead of Satan? You're on the right road, my friend, if this is so.

First John 1:9 says, "If we confess our sins …" *Confess* means to agree with God that what you've done is wrong. You agree with God that your lifestyle has been sinful and ugly. When, in your heart, you confess this sin of keeping the Lord Jesus at a distance, "He is faithful and just to forgive us our sins and to cleanse us from all unrighteousness."

Have you ever wept over your sin?

I can still see her sitting in a youth group meeting one night. I was speaking on this very subject, and she began to have a revival service right there within her heart. She became broken. Oh what a beautiful sight! She could barely talk after the meeting, but she tried to tell me what she had done. She had confessed her coldness of heart to the Lord that night and had returned to His loving embrace. Her best Friend, the Lord Jesus Christ, eagerly received her back into His mercies. The stiff-arm was no longer in the direction of the Lord; it began to be turned in the direction of the enemy, Satan.

Would you come to that place right now, teenager? Right now, fully embrace Him, His Word, and His plans for your life. Don't stiff-arm the Lord. Embrace Him again; He eagerly waits for you.

Read Matthew 26:30–75

CHAPTER 10

Things Have Wings

It was foolish what we used to do as kids. Always around Independence Day, it seemed we had an abundance of fireworks. Don't you? Now don't misunderstand, I don't think it was foolish that we had firecrackers, bottle rockets, roman candles, smoke bombs; things that rattle, smoke, and explode. Actually those things can all be sort of fun. What was foolish was when we started having contests among us as to how long we could hold a firecracker in our hands, throwing it away from us just at the last moment before it exploded. I'm sure that if you could have filmed (videotaped) our actions and then reviewed it in slow motion, there were times when the old "Black-Cat" firecracker was exploding just microinches from our fingers. *Foolish!* It was crazy! Some would consider it stupid. I simply use the word again—foolish!

Have you done things that are considered foolish? Sure you have. As we look back on our life, we all can remember those silly actions we did when we weren't thinking right. Actually, teenager, you'll find, as the years go by and you enter into adulthood, that you'll be amazed at some of the foolish things you did as a child or as a teenager. That's what maturity will do for you—it changes your outlook on what was good or bad, helpful or hurtful, wise or foolish.

Today we usually use the word *foolish* when we are referring to something that is considered silly or funny or "a little off the wall." When we refer to something we did years ago as a foolish action, a corresponding smile creeps up on our faces. However, I need you to change gears with me now!

You see, there is a time when God calls someone a fool—and it is not a laughing matter, not even a smiling matter. Whenever God calls someone a fool, there is no corresponding laughter. No sir, it's serious business.

In Luke 12:13, a man approached the Lord Jesus asking for help with regard to the disbursement of goods that belonged to him as a result of an inheritance. The man didn't have a clue about what was most important to the Lord Jesus. He assumed that this great Preacher of Righteousness could help him get his material goods from a brother who wouldn't give him his rightful due. This man's little world of self had put him on the short end of the monetary stick, so he approached the Lord Jesus to solve it for him. He simply wanted Jesus to make his brother give him the money. Yet it simply wasn't worthy of our Lord's attention.

Jesus turned to the man and spoke directly to him and said that He was not sent to deal with such legal matters. Then the Lord Jesus turned to the entire crowd that was following Him and used this man's question as an opportunity to teach them about *things!* He spoke on covetousness.

What Is Covetousness?

Before we go on with the story Jesus told, let's make sure we have a handle on this Bible word we've probably heard many times, but don't really understand: *covetousness:* What is it? Covetousness is the heart of discontent! It is when we simply don't believe we have enough of whatever we crave! We get caught up in what we don't have or what others have that we want, and we become discontented with our lives. We start craving more things. It is an itch that somehow won't go away. And it stinks in the life of a true follower of Jesus Christ.

Teenager, when you look at other young people and see their clothes, their cars, their popularity, their whatever—does it rip you up inside? Are you daily spending time meditating on the things you wish you had? You wish you had more musical ability, more athletic ability, more money to go and do as you desire, more shoes, more clothes, a car, a better car, more attention from a certain someone who has caught your eye, more freedom to come and go, more computer games, more laughs, etc., ad infinitum.

You are a covetous person! Pure and simple, you've fallen for the oldest trick in Satan's bag. It was covetousness that got him and his followers kicked out of heaven! Lucifer wasn't satisfied with what he had, his privileges with God, so he fought to have more. Is that what you are doing? You're in the wrong crowd, my friend.

Okay, let's get back to our Bible story from the Lord Jesus. Jesus turned away from the man who wanted his portion of the inheritance and faced the crowd following Him. Jesus then began to tell this story (see Luke 12:16–21): There was a farmer who became quite successful in his business. In fact, his farm brought forth quite a bit of agricultural benefits. The farmer looked at his existing barn and realized that he didn't have enough room to store all his grain and benefits from his successful farmland. Therefore he built bigger barns in order to carefully store everything. Smart move, don't you think? He was merely being a good caretaker of his agricultural accomplishments.

So far, so good. Yet here comes the problem. The man looked at all that he now possessed, saw the financial plenty that came his way, and declared to himself, "Soul, thou hast much goods laid up for many years; take thine ease, eat, drink and be merry." The words he used were spoken in such a way as to mean that he was planning for a lifetime of taking it easy. Evidently, his farm had made him a very rich and seemingly secure man. He looked at all his belongings and declared, "I've got everything I've ever wanted; I'm finally free to do what I really want to do."

That was when it happened. God called this farmer, "Fool." Whew, strong language. Why did God call him a fool? Was it because he was rich? No! Because he was a wise businessman? No! It was because he had decided to live for the wrong things. He thought he would be secure and satisfied with *things!* God calls any one of us a fool if we do the same thing!

Young person, it is foolish if you think the actual gaining of things will satisfy you. *Things have wings!* What do I mean by that? I mean that things will never be enough. You'll always want more! More attention, more money, more whatever.

How I wish I could look you square in the eyes and let you know you will never be satisfied if you are longing for

- more of a girl or boy's attention,
- more popularity,
- more sports,
- more television/entertainments,
- more clothes,
- more money to do whatever you want,
- more stereo systems, or
- more computers and all their particulars.

I stop with the list, but I could fill page after page with the list of items that pull for your covetous attention. If you don't learn how to deal with this miserable matter now, in the days of your youth, you will continue to carry this into your adult years. You will drive your spouse, your children, your friends, and yourself crazy!

Okay, I know what some of you may be thinking. "Morris, is it wrong to have some nice things?" The answer is clearly, no! The problem, my young friend, is when things "have" you!

Here's a question for you: would your life fall apart if you somehow lost what you consider to be a "nice thing"? I'm not saying that you should jump up and down for joy if your car is wrecked. Let's be sensible about this. I'm asking you, would you be miserable if it was wrecked? I mean, totaled.

What about this: what if your close friend got a new dress or a new car or a new boyfriend? Would that just about kill you? Would it be devastating to you if someone got something before you got it? If so, you are living for the wrong things. And it will make you a miserable person.

> For from within, out of the heart of men, proceed evil thoughts, adulteries, fornications, murders, thefts, covetousness, wickedness … (Mark 7:22)

(Not a very nice neighborhood to find your covetous heart in, is it?)

> And even as they did not like to retain God in their knowledge, God gave them over to a reprobate mind, to do those things which are not convenient; being filled with all unrighteousness, fornication, wickedness, covetousness … (Romans 1:28–29)

> But fornication, and all uncleanness, or covetousness,
> let it not be once named among you, as becometh
> saints. (Ephesians 5:3)

Solomon wrote about his tragic effort to find peace and rest in his book called Ecclesiastes. You know what he said thirty-three times? "Vanity of vanities; all is vanity!" What else did he say in reference to his search for fulfillment and satisfaction in life? Ten times he said his search throughout the world brought him "vexation of spirit." He sought for joy and rest in money, in education, in houses, vineyards, pools of water, controlling people, having plenty of women around, having a large choir at his disposal … but none of these *things* satisfied! And they won't satisfy you either. Here's what Solomon concluded with:

Morris Gleiser

Remember now thy Creator in the days of thy youth,
while the evil days come not, nor the years draw
nigh, when thou shalt say, I have no pleasure in them.
(Ecclesiastes 12:1)

In 1994, baseball fans were highly bothered by the baseball strike that shortened the regular season and eliminated the World Series. Still, baseball owners attempted to have something of a season anyway by bringing in some minor league players. These were guys who weren't good enough to make the "bigs" yet. There were other men who were brought out to play just for the entertainment value. They had other jobs, but they were willing to come out and play the game of baseball for a few dollars.

You know what happened? These part-time baseball players went around the stands and thanked the people for coming to watch them play. They thanked the umpires (imagine that). They came early and stayed late. They never argued calls made by the umps. Why, you ask? Because they realized they didn't really deserve to be there. They had been given a gift to play a game they loved. Their whole perspective caused them to be thankful.

When you remember that you have been given the gift of life; and I hope those of you who read this also know for certain that you have been given the gift of *eternal life*, you will have a perspective change on life! You will realize that God has been extremely good and gracious to you. You are undeserving of everything He has given you. Quit your complaining! Quit your bad attitude. Quit your covetous spirit.

Put the Lord in first place. Right now, get on your knees beside your bed or chair and tell Him you want Him to be number one. Put Him first, or you will never be satisfied. Put Him first, or your search for satisfaction will continue. Put Him in first place, or—well, I have to say it: you're a fool!

CHAPTER 11

The Sin of Grumbling

Americans seem to take pride in it. We never consider it to be that bad of a deal. Everyone—and I mean everyone—does it! It is everyone's favorite pastime. We excuse it in ourselves; we blame others for indulging in it; and we even start doing it when someone brings it up as possibly a wrong thing to do.

Of course, I speak of grumbling. You know what it is. It's called griping, complaining, moaning; being irritable, "ticked off," or even "righteously indignant" (this is the Christian version). Don't misunderstand me. There may be times when sinful activity occurs around us and we are angered at the carelessness and apathy of others with reference to their relationship with God. Jesus upset the moneychangers' tables when He entered into the place of worship in His day. Moses was hot when he saw the ungodly practices of Israel dancing around the golden calf. Elijah was greatly disturbed with the constant instability of the Lord's people in his day. Obviously we must never become indifferent about sinful activity. Yet I'm speaking to you about this matter of grumbling, murmuring, griping, complaining about life in general.

Grumbling means "complaining with a sustained bad attitude." It must not be tolerated anywhere in our lives. We can't blame it on our parents by saying, "Well, my father always complains to my mother, so it is inevitable that I've just learned how to do it from him." We can't blame it on teachers or coaches or other instructors in our past. Maybe someone has mistreated you, but that gives you no excuse to become a complainer. You need to stop! Today! Let me see if I can help.

Do you know of any griping individuals in the Bible? How about Judas? How about King Saul? How about Israel while wandering in the wilderness? How about the prodigal son's older brother? I don't know about you, but I don't want to be in association with any of those critics. You talk about lives of discomfort; they were miserable creatures indeed!

Let's take a longer look at Judas Iscariot. The Bible tells us in the twelfth chapter of John's Gospel that Judas started grumbling about Mary pouring twelve ounces of a very expensive perfume, probably made from herbs of India. The cost of this ointment probably was worth a year's wages for common workers in that day. Wow, this was some expensive perfume! Here's Mary sitting, as a slave, at the feet of Jesus and pouring this costly perfume on his feet and then proceeding to wipe His feet with her hair. Judas loses it and starts grumbling!

Why? Where did this bad attitude come from? Look at John 12:6. "This he said, not that he cared for the poor; but because he was a thief, and had the bag, and bare what was put therein." It is obvious that John, while remembering the response of Judas, recognizes the *cold heart* of this man who would betray the Lord Jesus at a later time.

John called Judas "a thief." In other words, Judas had a double life. He was one way in front of others, but he lived a secret life privately. In fact, Judas's life must have been one of extreme torture internally. He was, no doubt, a very disturbed man since he was on the outside looking in. He was angry with such a little matter because he had a self-centered heart. He carried the money bag, and all he thought about was how he could have had more money if Mary had not wasted this costly ointment. It's an ugly life, this life of a double-hearted individual.

So he griped; he complained; he grumbled!

A teenager who lives in two worlds will reveal his heart's condition by a griping tongue! There is an awful weight on his shoulders, called unconfessed sin. Instead of confessing the sin, he goes on in his wayward condition, and it pours out of his mouth through words of grumbling.

As a youth pastor I used to take teenagers out to eat after a youth activity. It seemed to me so remarkable that if I chose McDonald's, some would get upset and complain, "We never go to Burger King." If I chose Burger King, they wanted to go to McDonald's. They were never happy. Yet I also noticed that those teenagers whose relationship with the Lord was strong never seemed to have much to complain about. They enjoyed whatever and wherever we went. Godly people are sweet-spirited!

Do you grumble about schoolwork; about food; about the weather; about something someone said; about your hair; your looks; your brother, sister, mother/father? What are you trying to hide behind? What other sin hasn't been confessed in your heart? Why don't you come clean today with the Lord?

Not only did Judas have a *cold heart*, but he also had *blind eyes!* He didn't realize what privilege he had being in the presence of Jesus! How prone we are to do the same! We forget

- how good God has been to us, and we certainly don't deserve it;
- that we have the means of prayer to take our burdens to Him anytime;
- that we have outstanding promises in God's Word;
- that we could live somewhere without such wonderful freedoms;
- that we get to eat more food in a day than some will eat in a week or longer; and
- that we have friends, clothes, money, a warm house, a pastor, youth leaders, a youth group, education, music, etc.

One Sunday at a church, I met a starting pitcher for the Atlanta Braves baseball team. He was a Christian ballplayer who had a very good testimony on the team. He had even witnessed to several other players. Anyway, he knew of my love for the game of baseball and invited me to come watch the Braves play sometime soon. I could bring my two sons along also, and he would provide me with free tickets to the game. I excitedly checked my calendar and found the only date that would work for us. It was going to be great. The Braves were playing the San Diego Padres on a free Thursday night. Wow! (By the way, I might add that these two teams were two of the weakest teams in the major leagues at the time.)

I drove two and a half hours to get to Atlanta. It rained heavily the whole drive. In Atlanta it rained even harder. My two sons and I sat in the near empty parking lot waiting for an announcement on whether the game was going to be played. Finally after hearing that the game would go on in the continual drizzling rain, we made a run for the will-call ticket booth where our three tickets were waiting. By the time we got inside the ballpark, we were soaked. It was a cold rain too. We shivered on row 11, right behind home-plate. We sat in the midst of a few family members who had braved the cold, rainy weather. There was hardly anyone in the entire stadium. The weather was bad; in fact, the two teams were bad, and this late in the season, neither team was planning on a trip to the playoffs.

Yet we loved every minute of it! We sat there freezing, wet, probably getting sick—having the time of our lives! Why? Because we chose to. It was a baseball game, man! We were going to enjoy it, if it was the last thing on earth! (I was pretty happy, by the way, because the tickets were free.) We simply saw the privilege that we had—to attend a ball game—and we determined to enjoy ourselves no matter the conditions. What would complaining do? It wouldn't change the weather or the play on the field.

Now listen carefully, teenager. You and I cannot control our grumbling tongues. James 3:8 says, "The tongue can no man tame; it is an unruly evil, full of deadly poison." You and I need help! We must have the help of the Holy Spirit each day of our lives to bring our tongues under control. Otherwise we will continue to grumble. Remember what the Lord has done for you, and ask Him to open your spiritual eyes to the truths and privileges of Christianity. We have no business complaining.

Let me give you some closing counsel. What do you do when there seems to be a legitimate matter of concern in your life? Since you can't grumble about it and remain in a right position with the Lord, what are you supposed to do? Here are some things to remember:

1. Take your complaints to the Lord *immediately*. Let Him deal with the people and the problems. You just make sure your own heart is right with Him, freeing Him up to take care of whatever issue is bothering you.
2. If given the opportunity to make a suggestion to another, do so, creatively and graciously. Be prepared, however, for them to refuse your input. Your confidence must not be found in another person, but in the refuge of the Lord alone! Judas wasn't making a suggestion; he was simply complaining. Don't get caught in the same trap.
3. Learn God's plan of character building in your life. These issues of concern that often lead you to grumble are sent to strengthen you and improve you. Wait on the Lord to complete His work of Christlikeness in you. Griping and grumbling only lengthens the lesson.

Why don't you read John 12:1–8 and Exodus 16:1–22 today? Notice the grumbling attitude of these people, and see what the Lord is trying to teach you today.

Your pathway: is it a pathway of griping and complaining? Are you constantly seeing the negative side of things? Does anyone really enjoy hanging around with you, or are you a constant critic and complainer? Why don't you get off the pathway of complaining and take your burdens and concerns to your Lord? Leave them there!

Purity of Heart

CHAPTER 12

"Excuse Me, Mr. Referee"

The sight is a familiar one. We've all seen it hundreds of times. It goes like this: The coach is on the sideline; he flings a clipboard to the ground and begins screaming a tirade of words at that man in a striped shirt. The camera catches him in action, and I'm glad he doesn't have a microphone on him.

You see, the bottom line is this: the coach has a question! Now obviously the question has a lot of emotion connected with it, but it is a question nevertheless. The question goes something like "How could someone like you, Mr. Referee, be so blind, stupid, and ignorant as to miss that call [or make a call, depending on the situation] like that?" We both know that probably a lot more expletives go along with this outburst. Usually the coach's arms are outstretched, the veins are bulging on his neck, and he is bright red in the face. He may even glance up and down the sideline to get approval from other coaches or players. The truth is he doesn't really want to hear the referee's side of the argument; the coach only wants to give his side of the story and would love to see the ref change the call on the field.

Question: have you ever seen a referee change his call because the coach screamed at him and called him names? Yeah, me neither. It just doesn't happen.

Here's what is happening: most coaches call it "working the refs." They hope that, the next time something similar happens on the field, the ref will hesitate to make the same call against this coach and his team. The coach is hoping to be treated "right" the rest of the game. In his thoughts, the coach believes that being treated "right" means "Don't call any penalties against my team!"

Just once I would love to see a coach, or player for that matter, quietly go to the official in a game and say something like "Excuse me, sir, could I have a moment with you? I know your job isn't an enviable one, but I need to ask you something about that call you just made." Okay, I know that sounds absurd, but wouldn't it be refreshing to see something expressed with respect? You talk about "working the refs." I think this would really work. Personally I'd be impressed.

What I've just described is almost laughable; it just doesn't happen that way.

Let me be more personal. See if this isn't closer to home. Here's a teenager sitting in his room when his mother calls out from the kitchen, "Son, can you please come take out the trash?" Maybe the boy is doing homework, watching TV, talking (or texting) on his phone, or just chilling. Whatever he's doing, this task he's been called to interrupts his life. Everybody is about to find out how big of an interruption it is.

What's the response? First the forehead wrinkles, then a large sigh and mumbled words that no one can hear. He slowly (emphasis on slowly) walks into the kitchen with an obvious look of disgust on his face. He wants everyone to know how much of a problem this is for him to take out the trash (or whatever the task may be).

Does this sound more familiar?

My teenage friend, forgive me for being so blunt, but you're on the same dead-end street that coach is on, screaming at a referee. You say, "What are you talking about? I didn't scream at my mother!" I realize that, but your eyes, your mumbled words, your slow walk, your countenance did.

It's called *disrespect for authority!*

I know how frustrating life and people and issues can be at times—maybe often. You would like to be able to express your side of the situation. There are times when you can certainly express your thoughts or even make an appeal about your schedule and other pressures around you, *but always with respect!*

It never, never, *never* works to be disrespectful: in words, in actions, in looks, in ignoring the authority, or even by talking to someone else derogatorily about your authorities.

I have sometimes spoken to assemblies of young people and had to wait several times for teenagers to stop talking among themselves so I could continue. Sometimes the teenagers are laughing about something altogether unconnected with the message I'm speaking about. There are other times when I've had to hope that a teenager would wake up in order to hear my message. Look, I know that I could be misunderstood right here. It's not that I deserve some kind of deep appreciation, but anyone speaking to a group ought be treated with respect. It actually shows maturity on your part when you do.

You've probably heard about Samson in the Bible, haven't you? You probably also know about his moral failures, but his downfall actually started at home where he was rude to his parents. You can read all about it in Judges 14:1–3.

Hophni and Phinehas ignored their father, Eli, and it eventually helped bring the country of Israel into a tragic condition before God (1 Samuel 2:25).

Aaron and Miriam, the brother and sister of Moses, spoke disrespectfully to him and questioned his authority. Miriam was struck with leprosy, and Aaron was heard pleading for mercy (Numbers 12:1–10).

Would it help to tell you about Cain's disrespect toward his brother Abel but ultimately toward God; how about Korah's disrespect of Moses or how about those teenagers slain by bears as a result of disrespectful talk of Elisha?

How about you?

Okay, let's get down to business. You must learn now, while on the pathway of your youth, to respect authority. Speak with graciousness in your voice; seek no revenge, and stop thinking that you can change things by feeling sorry for yourself and being disrespectful.

How refreshing it is to be around a teenager who looks an adult square in the eye and obeys with a good attitude. This almost sounds like a strange, weird person who doesn't really exist, doesn't it? I've got news for you: they do, and you need to join their ranks.

They sit up close in church; refuse to be distracted by anyone or anything; and respectfully listen to the Word of God being proclaimed. They even keep their heads bowed and eyes closed worshipfully during prayer. In other words, they've learned to be respectful.

Examples:

I could tell you of Daniel, who was in a foreign country. He spoke with respect toward authorities and was rewarded for it. He rose to great power and authority in the Babylonian kingdom.

We could look at the life of David, who treated his parents with respect (1 Samuel 17:15–20) and even went on to be reverent toward an angry king.

The greatest example of course would be the Lord Jesus. He honored his parents on earth and ultimately His Father in heaven by going obediently to the cross of Calvary (Philippians 2:5–8).

Now, what about you? Be honest with yourself, how are you doing in this area of the pathway? How do you speak to teachers? How do you listen to preachers? How do you obey your parents? I know you've got a story to tell in order to explain away your need to be respectful. Just hang on to your story, and remember how Daniel, David, and certainly Jesus were treated. They all had a story, but they remained respectful!

Have you been recently guilty of the old "rolling of the eyes" which says, "This person really bugs me"?

I can tell you from many examples of teenagers I've known that being a respectful, reverential, and appropriate teenager is not only possible but a blessed way of living.

I can see so many young people who constantly express gratitude for their parents, teachers, and preachers. I can see them sitting in a location where they might listen and grasp a message being proclaimed by a pastor without much distraction. I can see them respond with private prayer after allowing the Lord to speak to their heart from a Bible message.

Many times this kind of teenager becomes one of the most respected young persons in their school and church. At times they have even received honors and awards at the end of their high school years. Then it isn't any surprise that they confer with their caring parents regarding college plans before stepping out of the home. This kind of teenager will see God's protection, God's guidance, and God's blessings in more ways that I can enumerate, all because they've learned to live with respectfulness.

Once again take a look at the life of Daniel (Daniel 6:1–24) and discover how he responded to those who obviously mistreated him. You will also be reminded how God delivered him and brought him to greater respect from others.

Check your pathway: are you traveling on the road of disrespect? Turn around—now.

CHAPTER 13

Stupid Samson

There's another area that needs to be addressed when it comes to the matter of walking in the right direction. It seems that young people just don't get much help in this area these days. Please stay with me. Hear the message; heed the message; head in the right direction!

I've done some really goofy things in my lifetime, and if you are honest with yourself, you'd have to admit the same. We have all done some real silly, foolish, ridiculous, stupid things in our lives. I heard about a teenage boy who attempted to walk on his church's balcony *railing* from one end to the other. Can you imagine with me for a moment the chance this boy was taking? He could actually fall onto church pews on the floor some twenty feet below with one misstep. *You would think he would have thought!* Looks to me that he would have realized he could kill himself or break some bones, do some permanent damage to himself, etc. But no, there he was trying to do the tightrope thing on a church balcony railing. Forgive me, but that's foolish; it's stupid. We can laugh about it somewhat, but it was still dumb!

There's nothing to laugh about when you study the life of Samson in Judges 14–16. Here was a guy that was born in a good home, had been taught from childbirth about Israel's God, and had actually been used of God to help others from time to time. You know when I was a small boy I thought that Samson was the first man who ever looked like these wrestlers that are on performance enhancement steroids. But that wasn't true at all. He looked like any other man in his day because the Philistines, Israel's enemy, were always attempting to find out what the secret of his strength was.

You probably remember how Samson eventually wound up in a dungeon with his two eyes poked out and doing the work of a donkey, grinding meal for the Philistines. What a miserable condition! He had to endure the taunts and hear the jokes of the enemy daily. He was mistreated as he walked in a circle all day long, tied to a grinding mill post. How did he get here? What went wrong?

It actually started in his home when he rudely spoke to his parents about wanting a particular Philistine girl to be his wife. His parents tried to get him to think straight, but he had his mind made up; he wanted her, "for she pleaseth me well." So we see that Samson had a problem with being submissive at home—which led to his more obvious problem with moral issues. Simply put, when you think of Samson, you can't help but think about his problem with his flesh; his lust for women. He had a morality problem.

My wife has this china cabinet in our home; it's called a hutch. Don't ask me what that means; I just know that is where we keep our china dishes displayed. It's good that we display those dishes since they cost so much. They are actually quite attractive and delicate and worthy of being on display. Ask any mother, wife, or girl, and she would tell you so.

Whenever we actually use those beautiful and delicate dishes, we never place them in our dishwasher afterwards. Oh no, they are individually washed by hand in hot soapy water. Then they are gently dried individually and carried back to their display case. But let me ask you this: what do you do with a paper plate after it's been used? With the exception of a few guys I've known that would try to eat the paper plate, most of us would simply throw them away, right?

Did you know, teenager, that when you give yourself over unto any practice of immorality, you put yourself into the position of feeling like a paper plate? You feel like things would be better off if you simply threw yourself away. This isn't true, of course, not at all. You're not a worthless paper plate or any kind of trash. It's just that Satan wants you to feel that way; and he has done a good job at making many people feel worthless. You no longer feel attractive; you no longer sense any value or worth to your life.

This is why so many teenagers have attempted suicide, trying to cover the guilt in their heart. Others have pursued other arenas of sin, thinking that it would help to cloud the guilt of immorality. Many times anger and bitterness walk hand in hand with immorality. You see it in Samson; you see it in David when confronted by Nathan the prophet; you see it in the illustration of Esau as explained in Hebrews 12:16–17.

Listen, temptation is something we all face! Even Jesus faced temptations of the flesh. Look at Hebrews 4:15: "For we have not an high priest which cannot be touched with the feeling of our infirmities; but was in all points tempted like as we are, yet without sin."

To be tempted is not a sin; to fall into temptation's trap *is* sin!

Temptation to be immoral comes in various ways. It may be something you are pursuing through the Internet, looking at various pornographic sites. It may be through conversations with other guys or girls. You may be viewing television programs, renting DVDs, listening to sensual music, reading suggestive material—I don't know exactly what you are doing, but I know that Satan is working overtime to get you, teenager! You can be sure of that. He wants to destroy your morals, your future marriage, your ministry, your mind. He will do anything he can to get you to that paper-plate mentality.

Temptation to be immoral is *strong*: somewhere between seven thousand and eight thousand young people lose their purity every day in America. It is considered a joke to remain a virgin in many circles.

Temptation to be immoral is *sustained*: there is no letup in sight. You can't even go through a grocery store line without being bombarded with magazines that have suggestive pictures and words on them.

Temptation to be immoral is *strategic*: the devil knows exactly what he is doing. He makes avenues of immoral practices accessible everywhere we look these days. You may even think that no one knows what you are viewing and doing. But God knows!

Let me get practical with those of you who sincerely want help. Please remember, regardless of what's in your past, God isn't through with you. I sincerely mean that. Christ died for your sins, all of them; I can think of no better news. God can forgive and will forgive you if you genuinely come to Him with a broken and contrite spirit. See your sin as God sees it.

But now, let me give you some practical tips on how to remain pure from this day forward:

1. Realize God Has a Better Plan

In Genesis 2 God created the woman for the man (one man/one woman). This is God's plan for marriage—your future marriage! Don't monkey around with God's design. You won't be sorry if you wait on God's choice mate for you.

Hebrews 13:4 says, "Marriage is honourable in all, and the bed undefiled: but whoremongers and adulterers God will judge." God wants a couple to enjoy the bliss of physical intimacy in the boundaries of marriage. So wait!

In Psalm 84:11 we read, "no good thing will He withhold from them that walk uprightly." God will bless you with a healthy, holy, happy marriage someday, if you'll realize His plan is better; way better than anything you could come up with.

2. Recognize God's Protection

God attempted to warn Samson that he was following the wrong trail when he headed down to the Philistine country for a woman. God sent a lion to attack Samson. Sounds crazy, but as Samson walked down through the vineyards of Timnath (a place of temptation in itself, since he was under a Nazarite vow and would not take anything from the fruit of the vine), God sent a lion to startle and awaken Samson. With the strength God gave him, Samson killed the lion with his bare hands. He should have stopped on the side of the road and recognized that God was warning him about the direction of his life; he then should have turned around and gone home.

It could be that God is using this very chapter to serve as a warning to you right now. God always provides a way out; an escape from temptation. (1 Corinthians 10:13).

3. *Run!*

I'm serious about this. Run away from any and every temptation that is knocking at your heart's door. First Corinthians 6:18 puts it bluntly: "Flee fornication." This means, "Get out of the neighborhood."

In the book of Proverbs a loving father warns his son by telling him to look out for the temptress. In Proverbs 5:1–8 the father closes a stern warning about the effects of immoral behavior by stating this: "Remove thy way far from her, and come not nigh the door of her house."

The greatest example of course would be that wonderful young man named Joseph. He almost seemed super-strong, didn't he? He would not fall for the daily attack and sustained effort of a seductive woman offering herself to him for sensual purposes. Well, you may think Joseph was strong, but I think he understood just how weak he might be. Why? Because he *ran* out of the house when she tempted him! He knew the natural bent of his flesh. Instead of talking his way out of it, he ran for all he was worth. He realized God had a better plan for him (he got married later on and had two children); he recognized a way out and ran!

Someday when you walk down the marriage aisle or come out of a side room to watch your bride walk down the aisle on the day of your marriage, will you be able to present a holy and pure life to your bride or groom? May you be able to look him (her) in the eye and communicate this: I kept pure for you; I kept my hands off of others for you; I kept my eyes off of sensual images for you; I kept my heart just for you!

If you couldn't say yes to those statements because of past failures, why don't you confess to your Lord that you are sorry, genuinely sorry for what you've done? You may need to get the assistance of a godly, loving mom or dad, maybe your pastor or youth workers to help you through the process of confession and to give you a plan to stay clean and pure from this day forward.

A college-age young lady approached me one morning at a youth camp several summers ago. I didn't recognize her, but she simply said, "I wanted to say thank you." I told her she was welcome, but for what? She began to tell me how, several years earlier, at another camp I had challenged a room full of teenagers to keep pure for their future spouse, for the glory of God. She went on to say that she gave herself to her Lord that night and declared that she, with His help and strength, would remain pure for her future husband. She said, "I never got to tell you back then about my decision, but I wanted to let you know today."

I asked her if she felt it had been a good decision and if things were going well for her as a result of it. She then showed me the lovely engagement ring on her hand and said that she would be getting married in a few more months. She was going to be a preacher's wife; actually a youth pastor's wife. Many months later

I was preaching in a church in the South, and there, sitting among several rows of teenagers, was that young girl, now married to her youth pastor husband, with a huge smile on her face. She made the right decision; will you?

CHAPTER 14

Calm in the Midst of Chaos

If you are a football fan, I mean a serious fan, you've probably noticed something fairly consistent with successful teams. This is it—there's an athletic and accurate leader called the quarterback. While bodies are flying all around him, people colliding into each other, a wall of blockers crashing around him and defensive players straining to tackle him, sweat pouring down his face, coaches and fans screaming in the distance—there he is, remaining calm and looking downfield to pass the football to an open receiver. Every coach will tell you without hesitation that he wants his quarterback to be that calming voice in the huddle, confident that they as a team can accomplish the task at hand, which is of course to score another touchdown.

We live in a fury-filled, fast-paced world with people in a constant flurry of activity. Many times we get caught up in the whirlwind of day-to-day living and lose control of our emotions. When that happens, we usually say or do something we shouldn't.

Are you familiar with the life of Joseph in the Old Testament? If there was ever someone that came from a dysfunctional family, it was Joseph. His brothers hated and envied him. They sold him off into slavery, telling their father that Joseph must have been brutally killed by a wild animal. Joseph became a slave boy in another country where he didn't understand their language, diet, or dress. As the years passed, he was lied about and was placed in a prison for several years. It would be easy imagine how angry and bitter Joseph might become. In fact you might even excuse him for being furious at his brothers for treating him as they had, which led him into such pathetic conditions.

Yet years later, Joseph was delivered from the prison and miraculously given authority in the kingdom of Egypt, at that time the most powerful nation in the world. He then had the opportunity to care for his needy family during an awful time of famine. You see, Joseph's brothers came down to Egypt, bowed their knees before the rulers of the land, and asked for food during the season of terrible need. Little did they know that they were asking for help from the very brother they had sold off into slavery twenty-two years earlier. You would think that Joseph would take advantage of the opportunity to get revenge on these men who had hurt him many years before.

However, Joseph did just the opposite. He wept over them, fed them, and provided for them, seeing that all of their needs were met. Wow, what forgiveness, what mercy, what grace—what a man Joseph was.

Teenager, are you an angry person? Do you find yourself getting angry a lot at people who get in your way? Do people irritate you? I'm talking about teachers, parents, leaders, and former and present friends. Listen to what Proverbs 14:17 says: "He that is soon angry dealeth foolishly." Ecclesiastes 7:9 says it very similarly: "Be not hasty in thy spirit to be angry: for anger resteth in the bosom of fools."

You might think that Joseph had a right to seek revenge on his brothers. Or he at least could have made sure they recognized that he had suffered a great deal because of them. Maybe he could have bragged on himself to his brothers just to let them know how great a person he really was. None of the above took place. In fact, Joseph asked this question in Genesis 50:19: "Am I in the place of God?" Joseph knew he had no right to seek revenge on anyone.

Is there someone you're angry with today? Is there someone you can't talk to and look them square in the eye with a calm, forgiving demeanor? Is there someone who angers you when their name is simply mentioned? Think about it—is there?

Sometimes we like to *blow up* and let the whole world know how angry we are. We throw things around, pound the wall or desk with our fists, and scream out words that let everyone know how furious we are. We have all heard stories about someone getting so angry that they actually express their fury with a gun or some other object that can inflict pain. Some young people have actually shot and killed their parents in a fit of rage. Anger is a deadly taskmaster that causes us all to do things that we eventually are sorry for. However, it is usually too late.

Then there are those who don't blow up, they *clam up*. They sulk, steam, brood, mope around, don't talk to anyone, and feel sorry for themselves. It's a subtle way to get attention and to let their world know they are upset without throwing a tantrum.

Then there are those times when we *spread out* with slanderous gossip about other people—people we're upset with or don't like. Either we make stuff up about people, or we add an emphasis about someone's life in order to make them appear bad or at least worse than we are. Here's the motive: if we can tear down someone else's reputation, it will make us feel good about ourselves.

What a tragic and low view of life we live when we think and act this way.

Why don't you *recognize* and *repent* of your anger and bitterness? Call it what it is—a sin that will lead you into further failure and sorrow. Hear again what Proverbs 14:17 says: "He that is soon angry dealeth foolishly." Start looking around at everything that you do have, and practice *rejoicing* at God's goodness in your life. It is truly amazing how things change when you focus on God's goodness and rejoice because of those things. Get a hymn book if need be, and start singing some of the familiar songs; you'll be shocked at the change of heart.

Then *run* back to the Bible. Find those passages that deal with anger issues. Spend some time in the Proverbs. Read the third chapter of James. Read some of the Psalms. *Remind* yourself of Joseph's example of a young man who could have expressed anger against his brothers when given the opportunity yet chose to do otherwise.

During my teenage years, one night I was angry because I had to work late on my job at a local pharmacy. One of my responsibilities was to deliver medicine to people's homes after their doctor had prescribed something for their physical welfare. One late night, working after hours, I had to make a delivery far from the pharmacy. This would make my time to get home much later than normal. I was fuming as I pulled away from the apartment complex where I had delivered the medicine. I muttered and griped as I furiously drove back to the pharmacy. I kept thinking how dark it was on the road that night. This added to my frustration.

Then at the very last moment I heard a scream right in front of my truck. Two teenage girls were passing in front of me between two curbs. I was driving straight toward them, in a fit of anger and rage, and hadn't even seen them. I jammed on my brakes, stopping just a few inches away from them; I probably would have killed them had I not stopped. You see, I was so angry when I got back behind the wheel of the truck that I had neglected to turn on my headlights. It almost led to two untimely deaths.

I sat in the midst of that street realizing what God had just saved me from. I began to weep and asked Him for forgiveness for my out-of-control anger. I began to see how good God had been to me. I rejoiced all the way back to the pharmacy and then on the way home. I've had to remind myself of that experience a few times through the passing years.

Teenager, are you angry at someone today? Are you harboring some bitterness toward a person you've known in your life? Have you been expressing yourself in anger? Why don't you repent of this right now, before it's too late? Joseph became a great man and one of the reasons for that was because he remained calm in a world of chaos.

Part Three:
Purpose of Life

Purpose of Life

CHAPTER 15
Scared

First of all I couldn't get anyone to even touch the casket, much less open it. Okay, I know it wasn't actually a real casket, but it looked like one—sort of.

Here's what was happening. We were having a church youth activity, and we were making use of the graveyard located on our church property. It was great for the purpose that I was seeking to accomplish. We were having a "scary" youth activity; whatever that is. It was amazing how many teenagers came out for this type of activity. We had a bunch of noises and scary events for the teenagers to observe and somehow experience. There was nothing tied to witchcraft, vampires, or the occult. Just good old simple fun-loving scariness.

Get the picture: I had someone build a box that looked like a casket. I would take small groups of young people to a dark location in the graveyard where the casket was situated. I would select one teenager in each group to go over and lift the lid to see what was inside. As I said, no one was willing to open the casket.

They didn't know it was empty. Once the casket lid was opened, I would declare, "He's gone." At that precise moment one of our adult workers would come around a dark corner to scare the teens. It made for great drama. It probably wasn't the greatest idea for a youth activity, but it was great to have so many visiting teenagers come to our church.

Here's the thing: I saw varied responses from the teenagers when they were scared. Some took off running; others froze and couldn't seem to move. One girl even fainted on us that night—three times.

People seem to respond to fearful things in their own way, but when it comes to responding to the work of God in our lives, it appears the response too often is the same. That response is a resounding *"No!"*

In Exodus 3 we are given the account of God calling Moses to a very special task: going back to Egypt, leading the Israelites out of slavery, and taking them to the land God had promised hundreds of years earlier to give them. No doubt, Moses was thrilled to hear that God was going to finally deliver Israel from their bondage, but he certainly didn't want to be the one leading them out. The job appeared too big, too hard—even impossible!

Moses actually argues with his God for twenty-nine verses in Exodus chapters 3 and 4. He tries to talk God into sending someone else to lead Israel out of Egypt. Bottom line? Moses was scared of God's call in his life.

Do you fear what God has in store for you? My young friend, don't get caught in the trap of fearing God's will for your life. On the authority of God's Word, I can tell you that He only wants what is best and will make you able to fulfill His will. To follow

God completely with your whole heart provides the greatest adventure of your life. Hey, when Moses got over his fears, look what happened; he became one of the greatest servant leaders in the entire Bible.

What was Moses most afraid of? The same thing you are most afraid of—*people!* If you will look at Exodus 3:13 and Exodus 4:1, you'll notice that Moses argued that *people* would make it difficult for him to do what God was commanding him to do. He feared what people would say, what they would do, what they would ask.

I've got to tell you the truth: I've seen many teenagers live their lives afraid of what others may say or do. I've watched teenagers stop singing in a youth service because of pressure from others around them who were not singing. I've seen teenagers avoid responding during a church or youth rally invitation because of a fear of what others might say or do. What a terrible way to live. You become completely bound up with thoughts of everyone else rather than obeying the Lord.

Proverbs 29:25 states, "The fear of man bringeth a snare." This simply means that we get all tied up in knots when we live in fear of what others may think, say, or do in response to our obedience to Christ.

Sometimes a teenager won't witness to another teenager who doesn't know Jesus Christ simply out of fear of being made fun of.

Sometimes a young person won't speak up for what's morally right out of fear of losing their friends, especially a boyfriend or girlfriend.

Sometimes teenagers won't dedicate their lives to God and become willing to follow His Word or His will. Why? Because they know the moment they give over to God's direction, someone will be there to question or belittle them.

However, I've also seen many teenagers stop fearing what everyone else will think about them and step into a new world of obedient surrender to their Lord. It always makes a huge difference when they do. You see, teenager, many other young people are desperately looking for someone to provide a sincere, godly example of leadership. Once you surrender to follow the Lord completely with your whole heart, others will also follow along. You'll never be sorry for surrendering your fears and trusting your Lord to know what is best for your life.

I watched a young teenage boy finally give his whole heart over to the Lord Jesus Christ, knowing that he would lose friends, be the object of mockery from some, and maybe even be cursed by others. This was no easy decision he made, yet he set aside his fears of others and surrendered his future, his life over to his God. Yes, he lost some old friends and was ridiculed and cursed at; however, he accepted it, knowing full well that things were going to turn out much better following the Lord. Today he has a beautiful family, and they serve together in a Southern city where he pastors a church. He would tell you that things greatly changed for the better when he got over his fears.

What is stopping you from full surrender to the Lord? Aren't you weary of a lukewarm, half-hearted Christianity? The rest of your life's chapters will be glorious if you'll set aside your fears, starting today, and give your heart and life over to the One Who has a great purpose and plan for you.

CHAPTER 16
This Is Your Kingdom

I love teenagers! I just love watching them live their lives and develop into the individuals God intends them to become. I was a youth pastor for many years and had the privilege of working with teenagers and their families. What pleasant memories linger with me to this day.

I recall one of the first times I realized how blessed of God I was to know and minister to some of the finest young people in the world. It was at a National Honor Society tapping ceremony in a high school attended by many of the teenagers I ministered to. I went to this school's NHS ceremony to see if any of the young people from our church would be inducted into the society. One by one several teenagers were introduced as new inductees into the society. Their grade point average, extracurricular activity, and overall character were being recognized and honored. Two or three teenagers from our church's youth ministry were introduced as new members. As their names were announced, the students would begin looking around at friends with that "I can't believe it" look. Occasionally the new NHS member would glance toward me for approval and a smile of acknowledgment. Yes, I was proud of them, much the way their parents were.

Then I looked around at the many other teenagers from our church who were not being inducted into the National Honor Society, basically because their grades wouldn't merit it. Yet I saw something else in them—*character!* Some of these teenagers were just as excited about their friends from church making it into the NHS. They were as excited as the parents and church leaders. These teenagers had average grades but superior character. I sat in great appreciation of so many teenagers I had the privilege to know, and to observe their character.

I'm not sure how Mordecai felt when Esther, his "adopted" daughter, had been selected to be the new queen of Xerxes in Susa, the capital of the Medo-Persian empire. Yet far beyond her beauty and charm was her supreme character. In fact, she truly saved the nation of Israel who were still captive in Babylon, even though Babylon had themselves been conquered by the Medes and Persians. This entire dramatic story is told for us in the Bible. You can read it yourself; it's simply entitled Esther. Obviously it is named after the queen. Seriously, this story is a page-turner. You see, an angry man by the name of Haman, had successfully plotted a way to be rid of the entire nation of the Jewish people in Persia. Mordecai, the stepfather of Esther, sent word to her to go before the king to plead for the lives of her family, her friends, and her nation. Then in his explanation to Esther he made that key statement found in Esther 4:14: "And who knoweth whether thou art come to the kingdom for such a time as this?"

In other words he was saying, "Esther, this is your time, your kingdom. God has placed you as queen for this day and hour. You are not a mistake. God had a distinct plan with regard to your life, and He has placed you in the kingdom for this time." No wonder Esther was able to reply with the statement she would go and stand before the king to plead for the lives of Israel, and "if I perish, I perish." So be it, she said—that's character!

There are several lessons for you to learn from this biblical account, but let's see this one big truth—

God Has a Time Schedule for You!

The Lord has always worked on a precise time schedule for everything: His birth, His death, and His future return. Even though we don't know when He will be returning, you can be sure He is coming again, and it will occur right on schedule.

But can I tell you something else that occurred right on schedule? It was someone else's birth—*yours!* Yes, yours! You are alive, right now, by the design of God. I hope that energizes you.

You see, you are vitally important to God! He has a will for you; that is, He has things to accomplish in your life. There are things you can do for Him that no one else in all the world can do. You are His distinct creation. You were by no means a mistake coming into this world.

Are you weary of praying for something? God has a time schedule for that; don't quit!

Are you weary of trying to find out what college to attend or even whether you should attend? God has a time schedule; don't become discouraged. He will let you know, in time.

Do you have questions about other areas in your life? Do you wonder about going into the military? Who are you going to marry someday? What kind of job or vocation will you have? Where will you live? The list is endless, to be honest. I'm sure you've got a lot of questions you'd like to have answers for. Guess what? God will let you know—in time! He has a definite time frame for these all-important areas in your life. Just remember this:

> This is your time on earth!
> You have been made for this hour!
> You are important to God!
> God has a special work and plan for you!

So trust Him—Esther did. Once she realized that God had placed her where she was, she accepted the fact that there was something she could do for her people. Therefore she walked into the king's presence and pleaded for her nation, and they were spared.

Picture yourself actually sitting in the stands at a professional baseball game, watching your favorite major-league team play. Then all of a sudden, the slugger on deck comes over to you and says, "I'm done, finished; it's your turn to go in." The look in his face is sincere. He states that his time on the ball field is over, and it's now time for you to take the next at-bat. I know this seems ridiculous and practically stupid to even think about. You're sitting there saying, "That would never happen; I could never hit major-league pitching." Now maybe you have some better idea of the realization that came over Esther when she recognized it was her time to "step up to the plate" and do what was required of her. It seemed impossible, but it was her time; her kingdom; her responsibility.

This is your day, teenager. This is your time to realize that God has a plan and work for you to do. It may appear difficult and practically impossible, but I promise you, this is God's plan and purpose for you. If you will open yourself up to Him and make yourself available to Him, He will show you His plan for your life. This is great news! Be thankful for it, and dedicate yourself to the task of honoring Christ with your life.

Read Esther 4 today and see the character of this girl. Recognize yourself in her example.

CHAPTER 17

Tribute to a Friend

Heaven has become such a real place to me. No, I haven't been there in my dreams, and I'm not morbidly sitting around hoping to go sometime soon. It's just that I've got some family and friends there. I recently had to say good-bye to a friend. He wasn't old physically; just an "old friend." You understand what I'm talking about, don't you? You have friends, some of them for a long time. Well, I had to say good-bye to an old school friend of mine when he died from complications of heart surgery. He was in his forties.

You never really say good-bye if you are a Christian and your friend or family member was also a believer in Christ. It's more like saying, "See you later; I'll see you there in heaven." Yet there is a real sense of memory that lingers with you.

I'm doing something I really have never done. I would like to pay tribute to a friend who has gone on ahead of me into heaven. Hey, don't be sitting there thinking I'm all gloomy and depressed. In fact, I'm a bit envious of my friend who is there with the Lord.

He gets to meet Moses, Elijah, Elisha, David, Daniel, Paul, and, of course, many other great Christians of the past. I'm not gloomy, so you don't sit there and get sad either.

Okay, I have to get ahead of myself just to explain why I'm talking about such a subject to you. I want to talk about friendship with you once again. You know how important it is to be a good friend and to have good friendship. One wrong friend can bring a lot of sorrow and bad decisions into your life. One bad friend can lead you down paths of destruction. Yet, one good friend can also keep you on the right path. That single person can bring a lot of fun, laughter, and spiritual growth into your life. There's nothing like a good and godly friend! Anyway, stay with me here, and I'll show you how this applies to you.

Actually, I don't really remember how I met my friend Steve. I don't know who introduced us to each other. I just remember playing tennis with him, going to church services with him, preaching with him on weekends at various churches where we had an invitation. We even roomed together in two college summer schools.

Our lives were filled with laughter and tears. Here's an example: One night I scared Steve in an empty, pitch-black dorm. The dorm was empty because it was summer and not needed. However, in that dorm was the Laundromat where Steve and I were to wash our clothes. I went ahead of Steve and hid in one of the empty rooms of the darkened dormitory. Steve knew I was in there but had no idea which room I was hiding in. It was hilarious. He came walking down the hallway calling out my name (actually my nickname, which I am not going to share with you). He was begging me not to scare him; I was laughing but trying to keep quiet at the same time. As he continued down the hall, I jumped out at the right time and simply said, "Hey!" He jumped out of his skin, throwing his dirty clothes all over the hall. It was a great moment and a great memory.

We also had some very serious talks together. In fact, there were times when we wept over passages of Scripture as we shared what the Lord was teaching us and preparing us to do for Him.

Steve had some outstanding qualities in his life, but let me share only two of the more exceptional ones. First of all, he had a genuine, caring concern for others. Any need of yours, when he found out about it, became his. He was marked by unselfishness. One night he bought fifteen or twenty pizzas so that every boy on his dorm floor could enjoy some. He worked at being unselfish and it came out in so many conversations, so many actions, so many things he did. He never gloated over beating someone in a game of basketball or tennis. He tried to make you laugh if he saw you were discouraged.

Second, Steve possessed a humble awareness of God's grace in his life. He never got over the fact that God was using him. He never felt he deserved God's goodness. He touched lives everywhere he went. He didn't feel worthy of opportunities to preach, teach, or receive recognition for things he did. However, he probably spent too much time comparing himself to others who were successful in some venture of life, causing him to think that he wasn't as good as others. While he was admiring others, they were admiring him.

Whenever I see teenagers taking friendship lightly or even mistreating others, I think about how blind they are to the value of friendships. Let me talk directly with you, young person. Please understand the preciousness of having a friend and being a friend. Recognize the shortness of the time you may have with others. Soon, your life with a particular friend can drastically change through death. This is your time to reach into their lives and truly *be a friend!* Quit wasting your time only looking for fun. Find fulfillment by living unselfishly for others. There are lives to be helped; friends who need your encouraging words; a person who hasn't smiled in a while waiting for the uplift only you can bring. You never know when you might help another person along the trail of life who may be considering suicide or simply empty of joy. I tell you this also, you'll find joy by giving joy to others. It's incredible: happiness is found by giving it away to others. Live for others and you'll find contentment in your own heart and life.

Jesus said in John 13:34–35, "A new commandment I give unto you, That ye love one another; as I have loved you, that ye also love one another. By this shall all men know that ye are my disciples, if ye have love one to another." What He was saying was that we are most like Him when we sacrificially give ourselves to others' happiness, serving them with spiritual and unselfish love.

So why not strive to be a godly friend? Don't just spend time thinking about laughing, hanging out with others, sitting up late watching television, or going shopping together. Come on now, isn't it time that you helped someone else grow spiritually? I mean, by just being in your presence, they ought to sense a need to spend more time with the Lord. Have you ever talked about the Lord Jesus in front of your friends? What would happen if you warned them of doing something they shouldn't do? As you are traveling through your journey of spiritual growth, take someone else along with you!

Thanks for going along with me as I've attempted to say good-bye to an old friend. I haven't done a very good job at it, really. However, if I can help you be a better friend, I feel it was worth the effort. Why don't you read 2 Samuel chapter one right now and hear how David spoke of his one good friend, Jonathan. Evidently their friendship was unselfish and meant a lot to both of them. David had to say good-bye to his old friend; he wept, he rejoiced, he remembered. Most of all, David was thankful for his spiritually minded, unselfish friend named Jonathan. I'm thankful for my old buddy also. I hope you will have the privilege of having a godly friend and being a godly friend also.

Good-bye, my friend; there will never be another one quite like you. Thank you for being my friend; my confidant; my prayer partner. I will never forget you, and I'm thankful I will see you again. Now that you are gone, I will work harder to tell others about that place where you are. You used to say, "Will you introduce me to your daddy when we get to heaven?" Now you have met him. When I get there, maybe the two of you will be nearby at the same time. I miss you, Steve. I am a better person because I knew you.

I'm glad for one thing, old friend. Now that you are in heaven, you have learned how very special you are and were to so many back here on earth. We miss you, but we wouldn't want you to come back to earth and leave the glorious presence of our Savior. God's grace led you all the way. Good-bye, my friend; my "Jonathan."

Purpose of Life

CHAPTER 18

What a Waste

I can still recall watching this kid play football. He was a natural; he had moves you can't coach. Not only was he fast; he was also quick. I watched him cause people to miss him simply by his ability to "juke and slide" all over the football field. He had natural quick movements which caused him to be a very successful halfback. He scored several touchdowns throughout the season until one night he was awful; simply awful. He looked like he was running in quicksand. He had no speed, no quick movement, and no heart to win the game. I think I actually saw him fall down one time when he was barely touched by an opposing ballplayer.

Something unusual happened that night after the game. Enraged, our coach dismissed this ballplayer from the team. It was not until the next day that the coach told us why he had taken the boy off our team. He had learned that the kid had been messing around with others who had gotten him involved with liquor and drugs. He was wasting his natural-born football talent by using illicit drugs and alcohol. I couldn't believe it. Why would this boy waste a talent most people clearly don't possess? I watched that boy around school, before he eventually dropped out, and said, "What a waste of talent!"

Yet I must admit, teenagers, some of you are very possibly wasting something much more valuable—your God-given ability the Scriptures simply call "the gift." You see, you've got to realize that you've been given a set of abilities that no one else has ever possessed. There has never been anyone quite like you. I'm not just talking about your fingerprints either. There has never been anyone put together with the abilities and giftedness that God has given you.

When you became a follower of God and accepted Christ as your Savior, the Holy Spirit moved inside of you and brought "gifts" with Him. He has helped to make you a distinct creation of God.

> Neglect not the gift that is in thee, which was given unto thee. (1 Timothy 4:14)
>
> When He ascended up on high, He led captivity captive, and gave gifts unto men … for the perfecting of the saints … for the edifying of the body of Christ. (Ephesians 4:8, 12)
>
> Now there are diversities of gifts, but the same Spirit. (1 Corinthians 12:4)
>
> As every man hath received the gift, even so minister the same one to another, as good stewards of the manifold grace of God. (1 Peter 4:10)

Without going into a lengthy detail please understand this, teenager: you've been gifted of God to help fulfill His plan for your life and to bring others to the Lord as well.

Don't minimize your gifts.

We have each been given something in our life, in our personality, in our mind. We have been given abilities in a combination of ways that make us creatures who can fulfill God's plans. There is no such thing in God's kingdom as "I just don't have *any* talent." You might think that you are incapable of doing much for the Lord, but you are oh so wrong!

Sometimes I think that some people state they have no ability and no talents just to get attention for themselves and to get others to feel sorry for them. This is clearly a form of pride and is an effort to get someone to supply you with compliments about your life.

However, there may be actual young people who have convinced themselves they aren't worth a whole lot to anyone, especially to God. Teenager, I can't begin to tell you how wrong you are in your thinking. Stop minimizing who you are and what you can become for God. It makes no difference what your home life is like, what kind of grades you make in your school, what seeming lack of physical athleticism is in your body, how poor your musical or other fine arts talents may be. It is simply that you have not found what your gifts are yet. It will come in time, I promise.

Don't maximize yourself (get an inflated ego) because of your gifts.

In some teenagers' lives, it becomes obvious earlier than with others what your talents and gifts may be. Along with that knowledge sometimes comes the awful smell of pride. Teenager, there is *no room for conceit!*

> For who maketh thee to differ from another? and what hast thou that thou didst not receive? now if thou didst receive it, why dost thou glory, as if thou hadst not received it? (1 Corinthians 4:7)
>
> For I say, through the grace given unto me, to every man that is among you, not to think of himself more highly than he ought to think; but to think soberly, according as God hath dealt to every man the measure of faith. (Romans 12:3)

I think it is clear that what abilities and talents you might possess falls into the category of "what I have is not really mine; I've been given gifts from God."

This means that we are simply managers, not owners. What we have belongs to God, not to us. We are to be busy for Him, not for our glory and praise. This isn't always easy to accept and understand, but it brings about a great deal of peace once we embrace it.

Don't misplace your giftedness.

What I mean by this is simply that far too often a teenager begins to think that someone else has a much better talent or gift and corresponding personality. Therefore one teenager starts to act like someone else, in an effort to feel good about himself. In other words, a teenager struggles to accept what he is and who he is. In an effort to feel good about himself, he attempts to act like someone else. You're misplacing your giftedness and attempting to do something or be someone that you're not. Teenager, this becomes a sham, a charade—it won't work! Don't compare yourself with others. Realize that God made you a distinct creation for His glory. Enjoy it and embrace it.

In the next chapter I want to help you discover and develop whatever God has placed within your being. But for now, merely recognize that who you are is a great thing. You were made by God to do a work for God. What a way to live; it's the only way to live.

A man inherited a large and valuable diamond upon the death of a distant relative. He traveled by way of a ship across the ocean to receive his inheritance. The jewel was so large and of such a beautiful quality that he carefully wrapped it in a soft cloth, laid it in a box, and then had it placed in a vault on board the ship.

One day on his journey back home the man walked around on deck and found himself thinking about the value of that diamond. He also noticed how bright the sun was shining that day and wondered how much more beautiful the jewel would appear in that sunshine. He then went to the authorities on board the ship, received his diamond from the vault, and went to a section of the ship where he could be alone. It was there he brought the jewel out of its case and observed its many faceted cuts.

He turned it around in his hands and watched the sunlight catch the variable turnings of the jewel. Carefully, oh so carefully, he tossed the jewel up to watch it turn in the air and catch greater beauty from the sunlight. It was breathtaking to behold. He continued to gain confidence with his tossing the jewel up in the air to observe its varied cuts and hues of light caught with each turn in the air. However, as he continued his game, the ship lunged and turned, causing the man to lose his footing at the precise time of one of his tosses of the diamond. As the diamond came back down, the man was stumbling. He reached for the jewel but was unable to make a secure grab. The jewel hit the end of his grasping fingers and began to roll toward the edge of the ship. As he frantically crawled and pulled himself across the deck, he only managed to look overboard as the gorgeous, costly diamond fell to its watery grave below the ocean. You can only imagine how sick that feeling was that came over the man.

Teenager, don't waste your life by playing loose and carefree with something much more valuable than a diamond. We're talking about your life here. God gave you His stamp of approval when He gave you His Son, Jesus. He has also given you His place on this earth when He gave you His set of gifts. You are of great value! Don't miss God's best for you.

Purpose of Life

CHAPTER 19

What Am I Supposed to Do?

His face was tense and wrinkled. He was looking back and forth between the brightness above him and the dusty ground below. He had just fallen off his donkey by some definite Presence, and now that Person was talking to him from the bright light above.

"Saul, why persecutest thou me?"

Saul was stunned and struggling with the obvious fact that he was not in control of the situation. All he could say was:

"Who art Thou, Lord?"

When the answer returned to Saul with the bold declaration that it was Jesus Who was speaking to him, Saul was genuinely converted; changed for eternity. He clearly accepted Christ on that road leading to the city of Damascus. His next question to the Lord was the question so many of you have possibly asked before:

"Lord, what wilt Thou have me to do?"

The natural question that occurs to a true follower of Jesus is this: "What do You want me to do with my life?" It's one thing to realize that you have been gifted by God to honor Him with your life; it is clearly something else to discover what you're supposed to do with it now.

Teenager, would you like to know what you're supposed to do with your life? Yeah, that's what I thought. If you seriously have a relationship with the Lord you, no doubt, desire to know what it is He has you here for.

Pursue God's Plan for You

This is what Saul was asking on the Damascus road when he asked, "What wilt Thou have me to do?" How do you discover God's plan, God's will, and God's direction for your life? What is it He has gifted you to do with your life?

Notice that God told Saul to simply "Arise and go into the city, and it shall be told thee what thou must do." In other words, God gave Saul a simple task—"Get up and go into the city of Damascus; you'll find out later what I want you to do."

Finding God's plan and His gifts in your life is sometimes made too complicated by people. You find God's direction for your life by simply obeying what is clearly understood. In other words, follow what you know you are supposed to do first; your "get up and go to Damascus."

It is God's will for people to recognize their need of a Savior first of all. When they recognize their spiritually lost condition and then turn to Jesus for the cleansing away of their sin, they are what the Scriptures say they are: saved. In other words, they have just become spiritually rescued. You cannot save yourself, no matter how hard you might try. Only Jesus Christ can rescue your eternal soul and bring eternal life to you. This is God's will for everyone.

> The Lord is … not willing that any should perish, but that all should come to repentance. (2 Peter 3:9)

Second, it is God's will for saved people to be baptized, showing others you have placed your trust in His saving work.

Then it is God's will for you to become available for Him to do whatever He desires with your life.

> For this is the will of God, even your sanctification …
> (1 Thessalonians 4:3)

What you are being commanded to do in the verse is to genuinely present yourself to Him, being willing to do whatever He tells you to do next. Take your hands off the steering wheel of your life, and let Him drive from now on. This is how you pursue God's plan for your life.

As you turn your life over to Christ and allow Him to be the Lord of your life, He will begin to place certain desires in your heart. Those desires represent His guiding plan for you. Any time you start believing that God will make your life miserable if you surrender your all to Him, that is when you start believing the devil's lie. God places desires in your heart and then allows you to have the fulfillment of those desires. You'll not find miserable people who are following God with all their heart.

Protect God's Plans

Can you imagine making a deposit of money into your savings account at the local bank and watching the teller take your cash and merely throw it over her shoulder to the floor behind her? You would say, "Hey, what are you doing with my money?" After she explained that she and the rest of the bank employees do that with everyone's money, you'd no doubt withdraw your funds and seek out another bank. You wouldn't trust someone or some organization that wasn't taking care of your deposited money.

Okay, it's a silly illustration, but just think: this is what we are doing when we don't protect God's investment in us. He has "deposited" certain gifts in you for His glory, for His profit. Don't waste your life and your future blessing by ignoring His gifts in you.

> Look to yourselves that we lose not those things which we have wrought, but that we receive a full reward. (2 John 8)
>
> Neglect not the gift that is in thee. (1 Timothy 4:14)

The mighty *Titanic* simply scraped across the giant iceberg in the North Atlantic. Small punctures, little pinpricks breached the hull of this huge ship. However, those tiny pinpricks allowed leaks that eventually sank the 95,000-square-foot ship.

Do you have some small pinpricks (unconfessed sins) in your life? Are there some tiny spiritual leaks in your life that are causing you to miss out on God's best for your life? Are there some wicked entertainments in your life? Some little lies, a little gossip, a little griping, a little bad attitude, a little playing around with sexual sin, a little spiritual breakdown?

You may think these are just small matters compared to what others are doing, but this is where you're wrong. This is also where you're going to miss God's best for you.

> Take us the foxes, the little foxes, that spoil the vines. (Song of Solomon 2:15)

Teenager, don't play with sin! Don't ignore this warning either! Don't attempt to pursue God's plans for your life without protecting God's plans for your life. Admit to God today that something is between you and Him, and confess it; clean it up immediately so you can move forward for Him.

Perfect God's Plans

Our friend Saul got up from his bright-light encounter with God, found his way to Damascus, and there learned what it was he was supposed to do. Saul (afterward called Paul) wrote that, later on, he went into the Arabian desert to spend some training time with the Lord (Galatians 1:11–18). He went away to allow the Lord to train and prepare him to better serve his dear Lord.

Later on Paul even told his friend Timothy to do the same (1 Timothy 4:14–16). He pointed out that if Timothy protected and perfected God's gifts, "thy profiting may appear to all."

Here's the point, teenager: Get to work spiritually! Start with daily time with your Lord, getting to know Him better. Ask the Lord to reveal Himself to you each day.

Second, look for areas where you can serve Him in your local church. **Sharpen your skills by serving with your skills.** If you can play a musical instrument, work at being the best for your Lord. If you have other obvious gifts from the Lord, improve them by using them!

It may be that the Lord wants you to serve Him in what is called "full-time Christian vocational service." This does not mean that you are better than others; it's just that you've been given gifts that He wants to use in His ministry somehow, some place. Be available to do so, teenager.

Whether you've been called into full-time vocational ministry or not, you've been given gifts for Him. Every Christian is to have ministry! Therefore, get busy serving and improving those gifts. You cannot imagine how fulfilling it is to know what it is He has given you to do—and then to do it!

When I was a young boy, my father taught me how to play baseball. He trained me to be an infielder, and I played on my first ball team when I was eight years old. I will never forget a game I was playing one Saturday afternoon. I was at my familiar shortstop position when a striking event took place. The opposing ball team had gotten the leadoff player on first base. The next hitter stepped into the batter's box to swing away. I was hoping that he would hit the ball to me so that I could try to get him and the previous batter out.

As I watched the batter swing at the pitch, I saw that the ball came off his bat into the air, in my general direction. I started declaring to my teammates that I would catch it; however at the same time, I noticed that the lead off batter that had been on first base was running toward second base. If I was going to catch the ball, he needed to make his way back to first base for that was the only safe place for him to be. I gloved the ball as it came down, snatched it out of my glove and threw it back to my first baseman. When he stepped on first base, the umpire called out, "Double Play"! Two outs were made on that one play. The ball team was excited, our coaches applauded their approval, but there was only one person I wanted to look at. He stood up in the bleachers that day; it was my dad, of course. I looked immediately for his approval. When the umpire made the double play call, I looked for my dad and saw his big smile and raised fist that indicated his approval. That was all I needed to see.

Teenager, one day when we see Jesus, all that will be important is seeing our Lord's approval for our life. All that matters is His approval. Live for Him today and each day ahead of you. Find out what it is He has placed within you to do for His glory and profit. Pursue His Plan, Protect His Plan, and Perfect His Plan, and you will receive His blessed approval.

Purpose of Life

CHAPTER 20

God's Nickname

Have you ever been given a nickname?—you know, some special name that your family, your brother, grandfather or even someone outside the family has given you. Usually it's some kind of a name that fits your character, your abilities, or even a spinoff of your real name. Nicknames can be fun to have, but we usually lose them as the years go by. When I was a youth pastor for several years, I was always dishing out nicknames to the teenagers in our youth groups. It was my way of having some fun with each one of the young people and a small way to let them know they were noticed.

There was an actual lady in the Scriptures who gave God a nickname. What I mean by this is that she gave God another name that fit her experience with the Lord.

Her story is found in Genesis 16. Hagar was a maid who worked for Abram and Sarai. Hagar was being mistreated by Sarai, so she decided to run away from the home and her responsibility. So often when we have problems with people or situations, we think the solution is to simply run away from it. This isn't true and usually ends up in further tragedy.

When Hagar ran away, she found herself out in the desert plains, suffering from the heat and thirsty for water and direction. This was when a preincarnate appearance of Christ met her in the wilderness and declared to her that she was going to have a baby and must return to the home of Sarai and Abram. No doubt Hagar's life was radically changed that day as she was confronted with the truth of Christ's care for her.

As Hagar was given guidance from the Lord, she turned to Him and gave Him His nickname; his additional name. Here's what she called him: *"El Roi"*—The God Who Sees Me.

It may seem strange to us to call God, "The God Who Sees" because we know that He does. However recognize the impact of this truth. Hagar was realizing—whether for the first time or not isn't important—that the Lord saw her—*really saw her!*

God Sees Me

Teenager, you may be thinking and feeling as if you are an overlooked, unimportant, insignificant individual and that no one cares about and even recognizes you. I've talked to some young people who didn't want to continue living, they felt so unimportant. This is exactly what Satan wants you to think. If he can get you to think that no one cares, no one sees you, no one even is aware of your existence, you'll start thinking there is no reason for you to continue to live. Learn what Hagar learned—God sees you.

It's a gigantic truth—you can't hide from God! He sees all that you are, all that you do, all that you say.

> The eyes of the Lord are in every place, beholding the evil and the good. (Proverbs 15:3)
>
> For His eyes are upon the ways of man, and He seeth all his goings. (Job 34:21)
>
> Behold, the eye of the Lord is upon them that fear Him. (Psalm 33:18)

There are times of loneliness, times of worry and fear, times of despondency and rejection. We all have experienced these types of emotions. During such times, you must remember and realize, *My God sees me. I am not forgotten by Him.*

A teenage girl sits in school feeling despondent. Her mom and dad are arguing a lot at home, and she fears that they are on the verge of getting a divorce. The girl feels responsible somehow.

She is struggling with her grades while others in the same class seem to get a handle on the subject matter without much effort.

She tried out for the cheerleading squad and the school's basketball team but was flatly rejected because of a lack of coordination. She also can't seem to play her musical instrument very well.

No one ever asks her over to their house and she never gets to hang out with any friends.

This girl goes home after school every day to the same old routine: she walks into her room, messes with some homework, practices some music, maybe has a meal, watches some TV, and eventually goes to bed—only to start the same old routine tomorrow.

What plagues many girls and guys at times like these is that they feel they are unimportant, insignificant, ugly, incapable, and especially ignored by someone of the opposite gender. The girl begins to think that she will never get married because "who would want to marry me?"

Listen to me—God sees you at times like these, but there is more to learn.

God Loves Me and Wants Me

Hagar realized that God not only saw her out in the wilderness but that He also loved her and wanted to use her in a mighty way. Her life was important to the Lord—and so is yours!

Hagar shouted, "God, You see me! I'm important to You; You want to use me!"

This will change your life, teenager, when you realize your value to the Lord. You are not a mistake with Him. You are not insignificant with Him. He wants you to pursue Him, getting to know Him. He wants you to realize that you are of great value to Him. He wants you! He wants you to know His love for you is real.

Think about it: He actually gave His Son Jesus to purchase you back from the claws of Satan. You are of great worth!

A little boy sat in a church service one night while a visiting missionary spoke about his ministry in a foreign country. The little boy sat on the front row with some friends, listening intently. As the missionary concluded his message, he challenged everyone in the service to consider surrendering their life to the Lord to be used by Him. He expressed that every individual in the crowd who knew Christ personally needed to surrender their all to Him. The missionary clearly declared each one's value to the Lord.

The young boy sitting on the front row seemed to understand, for the first time, that he was of some kind of value to the Lord. He took four or five steps forward, fell on his knees and began to pray at the church altar. He prayed a simple prayer: "Lord, I give myself to You. If You want my life, I give it to You; You can do whatever You want with me." With that stated, he stood up and returned to his seat.

You may ask if the boy ever became a missionary since he was responding to a missionary's challenge. The answer is no; however, he did become a preacher and a friend to teenagers. The little boy was me.

Teenager, realize this great truth today. You are seen by the Lord. You are known by the Lord. You are loved by the Lord. You are wanted by the Lord.

With Hagar of so long ago, why don't you declare that name of God in your heart? Call Him *"El ROI"*—the God Who Sees Me. When you recognize this, you'll recognize He cares for you and wants to use you.

CHAPTER 21

You Are the Light

It was early—really early. Something like 5:30 a.m. There I was, stretching out before a morning run. I had been coming to this park for several months, but this morning it was not only early, it was very dark; so dark you literally couldn't see beyond seven or eight feet in front of you. There was also a heavy fog that had fallen all around, which added to the difficulty of seeing where you were running. The bottom line was this, I couldn't see where I was going. I was trying to run around the park track, but I couldn't tell where I was half the time.

Then things got even crazier. I started thinking about the woods that circled around that park. I figured there were foxes, panthers and who knew what else in those woods. I started thinking they were all looking in the foggy dark mist at the crazy man jogging around all by himself. I also started wondering if they had enjoyed breakfast yet. I didn't want to be the delicacy of a wild animal. I know it was crazy thinking, but hey, it was 5:30 in the morning, and it was pitch black dark.

Little did I know that a friend had decided to join me that morning for a little run. In the midst of my crazy thoughts, in the midst of the heavy fog, in the midst of the darkness, my friend came up behind me. He simply cleared his throat as he approached—and I lost it.

The next thing I knew, I was down on my face trying to hide from the "wild animal" that was on the hunt for my hide. About the time I hit the ground the thought came over me that this might be a human, not an animal. As I looked up in the darkness I saw the form of my friend making his way on the same track as he looked for me.

Immediately I jumped up, let him pass by me (in the darkness) and then pounced on his back. I said, "Don't you ever do that to me again! You scared me to death!" I was smiling as I said it, and we both began laughing. He scared me, and I scared him.

Actually all of that occurred because of one major thing—the darkness.

You know, we take light for granted most of the time. We don't even think about it until we lose the electrical power in our homes, and we can't see in the dark. Remember when you used to have a little night light in your room as a little child? Maybe you still have a little Mickey Mouse light smiling at you in the middle of the night.

Okay, we've all be frightened in the dark before. Darkness can be creepy. It bothers us all.

You know what? The world is *in darkness.* When you and I were born into this world, we were born in spiritual darkness.

> But the natural man receiveth not the things of the Spirit of God: for they are foolishness unto

> him: neither can he know them, because they are spiritually discerned. (1 Corinthians 2:14)

That verse declares that unsaved people are unable to understand the Scriptures the way a saved person can. They are "in the dark."

> The way of the wicked is as darkness; they know not at what they stumble. (Proverbs 4:19)

Jesus was sitting on the northwest side of the Sea of Galilee teaching His followers when He declared in Matthew 5:14, "Ye are the light of the world." What was He teaching? What is He saying to you and me? What dos it mean to be "the light of the world"?

Understanding that the world around us is in darkness, we need to realize that the Lord was saying this: "You must recognize that you are My light in that darkness." In other words, teenager, if the world in darkness is ever going to come to the light of God's truth, it will be through someone shining the light of a good testimony around him.

A. W. Tozer said, "This is what you are here for: to glorify God and enjoy Him thoroughly and forever, telling the universe how great God is."

Can I tell you something really good? The Lord Jesus is saying, "You're important." He is giving us encouragement about ourselves. Now this isn't to say that we walk around thinking that we are better than others. No way! What I mean is this: He is saying, "I want to use you; I will use you; you are my light in this dark world; I will use you to get the light of the gospel (God's good news) to those who are in darkness."

Teenager, you and I are to reflect the brighter light, which is Jesus Christ.

> ye are a chosen generation, a royal priesthood, a holy nation, … that ye should show forth the praises of him who hath called you out of darkness into his marvelous light. (1 Peter 2:9)

I've met many young people who felt inadequate, incapable, insufficient, and insignificant. They thought they were of no value, but once they realized what they are here for, they began to reflect the glorious light of the Lord.

You may not be able to sing, but you can shine for the Lord.

You may not be the smartest kid in school, but you are God's light.

You may not be able to preach, teach, give a testimony to crowds, tell jokes, start conversations, or do anything else that you feel is necessary to communicate, but I'm here to tell you—you are the light of the world. This means you're somebody in God's plan!

But there's something else to be learned from this. You and I are to be shining in this dark world, telling others of the Savior that can change their life.

Have you ever done this? Have you ever taken the time to tell someone else of the saving work of Christ? Have you ever seen someone accept Christ as a result of you telling them about Him? If not, why aren't you shining?

If the world is in darkness, and it is, and the Lord states that you are His light in the dark world, why not start shining? Why not start looking for ways to tell others about your Jesus?

> Let your light so shine before men that they may see your good works and glorify God, which is in heaven. (Matthew 5:16)

This is a command, not a suggestion: start shining before others. There's no new way to express this; we're to go and tell others about Jesus Christ, His work of salvation on the cross of Calvary, His resurrection from the dead, and His plan to rescue their life from sin. We have the answer others need. The answer is Jesus Christ.

Right now you may be living with people who do not know your Lord. You may live near some friends, go to school with them, work with them, play ball with them, all of whom don't know your Savior. Isn't it time for you to start looking for a way to start a spiritual conversation with them? Start with asking them about what happens when someone dies. Let them give their opinions and thoughts. Then you can come back with this: "Can I tell you how I found out for sure that I am going to heaven when I die?"

By the way, none of that is going to happen if your life isn't reflecting Jesus Christ. If you aren't representing the Savior with your words, actions, attitudes, etc. most people aren't going to listen to your explanation of salvation. You've got to be a representative of your Savior.

> In the midst of a crooked and perverse nation, among whom ye shine as lights in the world; holding forth the word of life … (Philippians 2:15–16)

The teenage boy walked into the little market store at the end of his street to pick up some items for his mother. As he walked into the store, he was greeted by the bitter, depressed woman behind the counter who said, "Hello, how you doing?"

With that question, the teenage boy responded with great joy, "I'm doing terrific; how about you?" The clerk watched him with suspicion.

On another day he walked into the same store and the same event took place. He responded to the old woman's question with "Doing great, doing terrific; how about you?"

After this had happened five times—he had entered the little market and responded with eager and joyful delight to the woman's questions—she then retorted to the teenage boy, "Do you ever have a bad day? You always say you're doing 'terrific.'" With that question, the teenager told the lady that he, of course, had problems and bad days. The woman said, "I never see it when you walk into my store; how come?"

With that open opportunity, the teenager pulled out a gospel tract and handed it to her, saying, "Read this, and I'll come back to see if you understood it." The next day he entered the store and explained the gospel more clearly to the lady. Then he led her to pray a prayer of repentance and watched her accept the Savior.

How did this all happen? How was he able to lead a lady to the Savior? The answer is clear---his light was shining. His personal light of a glowing testimony shone every time he walked into the store, and it opened up the opportunity to tell the woman why.

Teenager, you can have opportunities like that too. It will happen if you'll start representing the Lord in your life. Realize that you are His purchased possession, give yourself to Him for His use every day, and ask Him to use you as His tool—His light.

Along the journey of life; along your every day's experiences; along the daily pathway—*your pathway*—

You are the Light of the World.

ABOUT THE AUTHOR

Morris Gleiser served as a youth pastor for close to twenty years, working with teenagers and their parents in two churches in Florida and Missouri. He also served as the director of a teen camp in Arizona for close to five years. He has written several articles for various Christian magazines and websites. He is presently serving the Lord as an itinerant evangelist based out of Indianapolis, Indiana. He has been married for thirty-six years. He and his wife, Lynn, have two sons who are both married and are faithfully serving the Lord in ministry.